First Steps Out

HOW CHRISTIANS CAN RESPOND TO A LOVED ONE'S STRUGGLE WITH HOMOSEXUALITY

Christy McFerren

With Contributions from Mike and Sharon Honea

First Steps Out: How Christians Can Respond to a Loved One's Struggle with Homosexuality

First edition: November 1, 2012
ISBN-13: 978-1480160347
ISBN-10: 1480160342

For Mom and Dad.

Without your love, the rest of my story could not have been written. You were gravity to me.

And for Dan.

For your indiscriminate, immediate, and intentional love which has not lifted since our hearts first met. If there were ever another more like Christ, I have not met them.

"But in all these things we overwhelmingly conquer through Him who loved us. For I am convinced that neither death, nor life, nor angels, nor principalities, nor things present, nor things to come, nor powers, nor height, nor depth, nor any other created thing, will be able to separate us from the love of God, which is in Christ Jesus our Lord." — Romans 8:37-39

Table of Contents

GETTING SUPPORT

Author's Note

Far from being a complete guide to all aspects of the topic of homosexuality, *First Steps Out* is primarily intended to set a very difficult and often unproductive conversation off on the right foot — in a new, life-giving direction. The original impetus for writing was the number of parents who, knowing about my journey, began to approach me about this topic asking for advice when their child confessed to struggling with same-sex attraction. Some of their kids had "come out" in decisive statements, while others simply confessed to being same-sex attracted against their preference. The title speaks to the importance of responding well to these situations from the start. The first moments are so defining in the overall course of relationship. As I heard of first responses to family members that made me cringe, I felt pain for these families because of the unnecessary damage being done through a lack of understanding. I've become concerned that uninformed responses are burying people deeper in mistrust and pressing people to run further away from God and into hopelessness. I want to help parents get off on the right foot as they take their first steps in dealing with this new information. The first steps of response are so crucial because they can become a loved one's first steps of victory over homosexuality.

In this book, I share portions of the story surrounding my twenty-three year struggle to overcome homosexuality intended to unpack what some people who struggle with same-sex attraction may be going through. Not everyone who experiences homosexual desire will be able to relate to my story, but many have and will relate. My parents also contributed to this book, offering their stories along with helpful perspective and insight on how they handled my confession and subsequently reconciled their love for me with their firm convictions rooted in biblical truth. We would never claim to know everything there is to know about this topic, but we share our lives as an open book with the hope that we can help prevent unnecessary tragedy by keeping families and friendships from falling apart. My struggle affected my family quite deeply, and we, collectively, can offer hope that receiving the news that a loved one is gay does not have to mark the turn of a plot into tragedy.

In addition to helping families learn what transformative love looks like in this situation, we're hoping to inform and educate the greater Christian culture in two ways. We want to see the Church equipped and empowered to better support the parents we're writing to. Tragically and far too often, the Church pins the blame on grieving parents' mistakes — whether real or perceived — lessening the likelihood that these parents will have strength to love well when it matters most. Parents, family, and close friends are often the only path people have to Church and God. It's important that we, the Church, learn to recognize those who are living as bridges to God for the gay community, and keep them strong and undergirded. Secondly, we want to build a framework of general understanding of same-sex attraction and homosexuality that builds a smarter Church so people who struggle with their sexual orientation might feel more at ease with approaching God.

The number of stories I continue to hear empowers my belief that there are not enough resources equipping families and churches to handle these situations with grace. As a result, hopelessness and apathy usually set in when this issue arises in a Christian's life. Families are being pressed to a breaking point under the weight of this still mysterious topic, and as of now, fear and lack of knowledge still rule the day. Adding to the pressure, the culture is lacking an advocate for those who struggle but ultimately do not want to accept their homosexuality as an identity or permanent condition. No one is telling these young people "it's OK to fight" your homosexual desires. The primary message of our culture is "come out and stay out." My suspicion is that there are more people who "come out with pride" than want to, simply because no one has given them permission to think outside that box and to "come out with questions." They come out because they can no longer bear the grief of hiding their struggle. If it's like my story, it's more about letting light in on dark secrets than it is about being rebellious. So let's offer light, and learn how to love them so we can be prepared to walk with them in search of answers when they do "come out with questions."

In summary, it's a delicate moment when someone confides about their struggle with same-sex attraction or similar issues — a moment our culture often fails to handle with grace. We're out to change that. We believe the Bible when it says love covers a multitude of sins, and we dare to believe that if families and churches can foster an environment of unconditional love toward this community and build refuge on the unchanging principles of God's word, change will come to the hearts who seek it.

A Special Note To Parents

If you picked up this book, it is likely that your heart is breaking.

I don't take lightly the opportunity to speak into your situation, and I respect you for your courage to educate yourself and deal righteously with your loved one's — perhaps newly placed — confidence in you. They have entrusted you with a very intimate and delicate personal matter, and they need your love and approval of them as a person.

Please do not withdraw that, no matter what you do, no matter how hard it gets, no matter how long this takes.

Love them. Please.

That is the bottom line of what I am going to be saying in this book.

Who This Book Is For

This book is primarily for the parents, grandparents, siblings, and friends — the community of trusted people — around those who have shared that they are struggling with homosexuality. You and this person in your life are most likely both overwhelmed by this situation. Perhaps they are wavering but not sold on embracing their orientation, or they are totally sure they want to be heterosexual despite their current feelings. If this is your situation, or very close to it, this book is written to help you get perspective on what they are going through, how to avoid destructive responses that create relational dysfunction, and how to be a positive voice for hope in their life.

I'm assuming you walk in the Christian faith, and that you will be drawing from its principles to guide you. The infinite patience and love of God are without comparison, and you'll need the fruit of His Spirit actively at work in your heart as you seek to be a refuge and strength to your friend or family member. It is my experience that with every new situation we face, the dynamics of Christianity don't change, but there are layers of revelation about these dynamics we don't reach until we find ourselves in the crucible of certain struggles. What I am going to cover could seem basic to people who are not in the midst of this kind of trial while being full of life and revelation to those who know this pain far too intimately.

To be clear, while not primarily written to them, this book can also be helpful to the community surrounding those who are decidedly homosexual and not looking at this time to change that. You may gain some perspective if that is your loved one's situation, but engaging in conversation over some of the information I share could be unproductive if someone has already decided about this issue.

Free will is a God-given right, and we cannot seek to override that, no matter how much we love a person and desire their choices to be different. It becomes a matter of prayer and faith for the loved ones of a person whose will is currently set on remaining in their homosexual orientation.

My husband has a saying I seek to remember often: *"No man is ready to hear the answer to the questions he isn't asking yet."* Said another way, advice without invitation is always heard as criticism. Further, when God begins to move on a heart about this or any issue, a person will begin to stir up the conversations vital to their journey, and we can rest assured truth will have its day in the sun.

Truth takes root and grows tallest in the fertile hearts of those who are asking for it and will tend to its maturing and application without pressure. For those not yet asking questions, unconditional love, prayer and faith are awesome and powerful gifts from God. They can go a long way toward seeding a heart to begin asking the right questions and moving toward change.

CHURCH and CULTURE

Why Listen to Me?

Speaking on matters of church and culture can be intimidating at best, especially when it comes to the topic of homosexuality. Strong feelings abound, and this issue has galvanized an entire generation. We are left with hearts strewn about and polarized opinions on every front. The conflict is very real, with its dividing lines running right through the Church just as much as the culture at large. Understandably so, people get nervous when we talk about this. We grow tense and gear up for a fight. No doubt some sweaty palms are parsing through these pages, even now.

When you take the stage in a scene like that, it's usually a good idea to give your credentials. You know, the string of letters that follow your name and validate your voice. And well... I'd have some — I tried, I really did — but I've spent most of my life fighting this and haven't quite made it through the ranks of higher education yet. I'm working on that. But let's officially get this out of the way: I am not a professionally licensed counselor, I am not a doctor of any sort — I do not even hold a bachelor's degree. I'm a thirty-something Bible school and art school dropout whose life was overtaken by this struggle before I could finish my formal education.

I just have my story. Street cred + the Spirit of God. That's it.

Contrary to popular opinion and political correctness, I am a testimony that homosexuality can be a choice. I am writing a separate book recounting my story in full, but for the purposes of this book, a condensed excerpt from it follows.

It was 1994. I was 15 years old when the epiphany hit me that times were changing and I was eventually going to have a socially acceptable problem.

This sudden awareness started the clock on a grueling battle for my sexuality. I was conscious of the fact that I was different from the other girls at the age of five, and I had lived silently through ten years of gender confusion and attraction to women by age fifteen. I wanted desperately to be "over it" by the time it was going to be acceptable, even normal, to be gay.

I've always been conscious of God.

My Baptist upbringing made me aware of my need to be able to give an account for all the decisions that added up to the story of my life. Sometimes a burst of scripture and the fear of God were strong enough to keep me in check. But, for most of my story, I just didn't feel like I was in control of the pen.

Years before I shared my struggle or had a single conversation about it, I knew the way I felt toward women was not only different, but wrong.

Deep down. Instinctively, I hid it. Like Adam and Eve, in the garden, when they got it wrong. It was not the topic of sermons or conversations in the early 90's. It was still foreign at best, if not taboo. No one influenced me to fight these feelings because no one knew. It was the voice of God alone that spoke to my heart and persuaded me to fight for my identity.

From childhood, I wanted a husband and a family. I didn't want to die in the arms of a woman at the age of sixty-four. Or forty-whatever. It wasn't about shame before men, it was about honor before God. I couldn't look God in the eye someday and tell Him I had tried to honor Him in every way He'd asked of me if I had given up easily when it came to this.

So I fought. Hard.

In my early teens, I told my youth minister's wife. In my later teens, I fell in love. Deeply. After being caught, her mother allowed me to choose: I could tell my parents in the next twenty-four hours, or she would. I couldn't let them hear it from anyone but me so I confessed my struggle to my very broken-hearted parents.

On a Sunday, I told them I had to move to make a new start, and I was gone by Wednesday. It ripped gaping holes in all of our hearts. It's not the way you're supposed to leave home, but I didn't know what else to do. Unsure what to do with myself, I followed up on some previously abandoned plans and went to Bible school in Dallas. After one semester, I dropped out and checked myself into a live-in Christian counseling center for people fighting homosexuality. I found out the program was inactive after I moved in, and after a year there, I got so lonely that I left and let go of the fight for a time.

Ready to pick myself back up again I enrolled in art school in honest pursuit of a web design career, but found myself swimming in temptation and unable to concentrate. I dropped out of art school to run away from another relationship that was forming, and moved to Austin where I enrolled in a school of ministry. A few years later, I found myself in trouble again, and had to step down from ministry. My teens and twenties were marked with cycles of victory and defeat, joy and pain.

Homosexuality is not a tender enemy.

But, I'm thankful for the affliction because it made a warrior and a lover of me.

For my entire twenty-three year search, I was never alone. When I made the decision to reach for help, people loved me. They prayed, listened, cried, and held me. They believed the best was coming and waited tirelessly for the seeds of life to bear fruit in my soul. By patient love they demonstrated my Father's heart. The best of them never violated my will, created forceful situations, made rules for me to follow, rushed me to conclusions, or prescribed remedies. They gave me no reason to mistrust God by their own leadership styles. They didn't make my sin any bigger than theirs. They didn't freak out when I fell. They just spoke truth, and waited with me until I could see God. Because that's the promise for the pure in heart. They see God.

During my struggle, I was at times almost overwhelmed by a relentless, internal pressure to make a decision that would define me in the long term. I contemplated "coming out," not because I was suddenly proud of it, but because I was tired of fighting... particularly after a failure. I was exhausted and humiliated. I wanted to disappear; not confess to loss again. Pride's temptation to turn struggle into statement, wrong into right, was intense. In these moments, depression weighed heavily on me. Vision for life faded in and out, like a boxer reeling from blows to the head. But I just wouldn't lay down on the mat and quit. It felt too much like making a deal with the devil. I knew the pressure to come out was a demand for my agreement with darkness, and would turn my heart to enmity with God.

At some point, the most important lesson of my struggle became revelation to me:

I don't have to make an enemy of God just because I'm not quite like Him yet.

I learned that more than angering Him, my failures broke His heart. I learned in order to please Him, my heart only needed to be in agreement with His. And to make agreement, I only had to yield my pride to His love.

I learned this: the entire battle... all these years... had simply been about my agreement. Profoundly simple, it was this revelation that removed the pressure to define myself as gay or straight, and gave me the freedom to be in process. It made it OK to fight.

I began to see that each time I made decisions toward truth, there was a positive energy around it, unlike the negative energy that would have me come out.

Rather than giving in to get relief, I was rising up to grasp hope.

Sometimes I agreed with God about my sexuality because He is Lord, and love is a choice, and that is all. My emotions were left out of the equation so many times because I had to believe either my feelings were lying to me or God was. I purposed in my heart to honor God's design no matter how it felt, for a very, very long time. I could feel in the waiting that Life was at work in me. Hope was at work in me.

There was never a pinnacle moment when I knew, "I'm not gay anymore. I feel different." My liberation was unceremonious. Freedom matured in me through a process, from the seeds of truth that God planted and people watered along the way. It wasn't one decision I made not to be gay, there were many. Like Proverbs 4:18 says, "... the path of the righteous is like the light of dawn, that shines brighter and brighter until the full day."

When dawn first breaks light is distinct from darkness, but its brightening from morning to noon happens in indiscernible progression. Yet noon is undeniably brighter than the dawn. In the same way I can say with confidence today that I am free. The darkness of midnight is untraceable in the midday sun of my life.

I am a testimony that homosexuality can be a choice. It was a fight, but it was worth every tear I cried and every drop of blood Jesus shed. We won this thing together. It was a fight for honor. For dignity. For agreement. Out of that agreement comes the power that overtakes the impossible, and if you're struggling with this, I'm here to tell you...

It's OK to fight.

After sharing this story with my largest public audience to date on *Prodigal Magazine* (http://prodigalmagazine.com/on-homosexuality-its-ok-to-fight) in August of 2012, I have been approached by more people than ever whose stories and struggles are similar to mine asking for more specifics. They want to know how I went from being attracted to women to legitimately being attracted to men.

Also interesting, I have been approached by heterosexual people who have never struggled with same-sex attraction, but want to know more about the mystery that is homosexuality. They're seeking to understand its dynamics and how a person can "get there."

Regardless of the background of those who inquire about my struggle, the conversation that follows both angles of questioning is mostly the same, and I find it to be a place where bridges are being built. Up to now, the inability to understand our differences has given place for anger and hostility to rise between the two perspectives, but I believe a new conversation is unfolding where compassion will take root.

I have a special place of compassion in my heart for people who want to love those who share my struggle but can't relate. With no frame of reference within themselves, it's sometimes difficult for those who have never experienced same-sex attraction to understand, and it's a challenge for their spiritual growth to actively love and choose not to view those who do struggle as intentionally deviant.

Those who are attracted to the same sex usually can't fathom an existence where it's not at least something of a perfectly natural temptation, and struggle not to view those who say they can't relate to them as unenlightened bigots. From their perspective, it is really hard to get your head around the lack of empathy.

I want to share more details about my process here in the name of bridge building. The roots of attraction may be a little different for everyone, so this is not intended to be an oversimplified answer that is applicable to everyone, but I've seen evidence that the more people who have been on both sides of the issue and are willing to share their perspectives, the better off our culture will be.

Because I fought my sexuality so adamantly, I was not in many long-term relationships with women, but there were a few women I was especially attracted to — enough so that I was willing to suspend my convictions and attempt to form a relationship. These usually lasted just a few months. The relationships were characterized by a kind of manic excitement at first with undertones of fear of abandonment and jealousy in place from the start. Over a short period of time, the undertones would become defining marks of the relationship, and I would hold the person tightly to myself with the sense that letting go would be losing not only them, but part of me. The relationships would become either a highly dysfunctional tug-of-war rooted in control and jealousy, or a symbiotic existence full of codependency and expectations that mounted too high for either person to achieve. In either scenario, disappointment and heartache were certain to follow.

In reflecting on the way my relationships went when I gave in to my same-sex attractions, over time I began to realize that the women I was drawn to were women who had either physical characteristics or personality traits that I felt were inadequate in my own expression of womanhood. For example, I was mostly drawn to bubbly personalities because I am a quiet and serious person much of the time. Or, I was drawn to petite women because with my larger frame, I never felt I fit the bill for what a woman should look like to be considered attractive in our society. When this first occurred to me, it didn't seem that wrong because even heterosexual couples seek people who complement their weaknesses. Opposites attract, right?

But I began to realize that I was seeking the missing pieces of my womanhood from the women I was with. Then I saw that anytime I was hurt by my partner, the pain was so deep it was as if my sense of womanhood was being threatened. I was controlling, possessive and expressed a strong need for agreement and affirmation because I had somewhere in the process looped this person into my identity as an inseparable part of me. Any action they took that indicated a distinction between us as people resulted in a fight. I felt either legitimized as a valuable person or completely worthless based on their everyday responses to me. It was an exhausting roller coaster.

When I first began to see and understand that this is what was at work in me, I started to rise up a little bit against it. The foundations of my faith gave me the understanding that I could and should call out to God for completion and identity in these areas instead of trying to draw it out of a relationship with a woman — or any human for that matter. The revelation came that I was engaging in idolatry, expecting wholeness and fulfillment from something and someone that wasn't designed to give it to me, and I was valuing that as primary to God. It was angering and humiliating when I saw that I was underestimating my own womanhood and allowing some other woman to define what was rightfully and uniquely mine to express. This marked my freedom from the bondage of looking to women for affirmation in my womanhood, and I started looking for that affirmation in the mirror — the one I dressed in front of each day and the one this is the Word of God.

I wasn't immediately changed entirely. The habits of my emotions and sexuality were forces to be reckoned with for sure (that's where the "fight" came in), but I was free from the trappings that would draw me back in with any real level of expectation. Freedom introduced a new level of logic I had not experienced in my struggle before, and as a result I never engaged the idea of a same-sex relationship again with any sense of merit or as a legitimate option for my life.

With serious gaps in my identity closing quickly, I began to see the appeal of having a man in my life. As time went on and my expression of womanhood became more clear and defined in me, I grew in confidence and began to look at men with new eyes. Over time, I began to evaluate what I would want in a man and it became very clear to me that I was certain my attraction to women had ended. I was in fact sexually and emotionally attracted to men. I never dated, but I was certainly studying the landscape.

After about five years of freedom working in me as a single woman, at age thirty-two, I met the love of my life on the Internet in August of 2011. We exchanged mountains of emails, totaling nearly one hundred pages of deep conversation with the expressed intention of determining if we were "right for each other." After a month of literally trying to convince ourselves the truth was too good to be true with disqualifying questions of every kind, we failed! We decided to meet in person in September. The night before we met, he remarked that he felt he was not meeting a new person, but reuniting with a long lost friend. Our meeting was the stuff of movies. We couldn't speak. He had tears in his eyes. I stared at him. We forgot how to order coffee. Our two-hour date turned into eight. We saw each other daily after that. Two weeks passed and he proposed. On November 1, 2011, I married the man God had always known would be waiting for me at the end of this very long path to reconciliation in my identity.

I feel satisfied to have overcome, and to have finally made peace with the gender I was born with. I feel complete with a man, as a woman. In addition to enjoying my marriage, I share healthy friendships with other women. I feel secure in my womanhood and identity, a holy intimacy is a reality, and the lines of moral propriety are clear. I wouldn't trade for the life I have now, and I never think about life in any other way.

After hearing my story, some have asked me if I really... never... struggle. It is true. Sure, as with anything we have left behind, I assume I could work my way back into my former identity. But I don't have to actively suppress it to maintain freedom. To the contrary, I would have to actively work to "find" that version of myself again. It's not alive anymore. I say this in humility, fully aware that it is merely the grace of God that sustains this reality, but I also say it with confidence, having come to know what I know about the strength of that grace.

It took me a long time to become willing to share my story or offer hope to those familiar with my footsteps. I didn't (and don't) want to become pigeonholed as a writer or speaker about this singular topic. I run so much deeper. I don't look forward to receiving heated emails and can live without being "in the fray" on this topic. I don't want to hurt anyone's feelings, and the truth sometimes does that. So it was my aim to marry, buy a house, raise kids, and hide behind my picket fence as it concerned the issue of homosexuality — it had already taken enough of my attention.

Until this generation, it has always been "someone else's" very odd, unique and shameful problem. But now, it has become commonplace for Christian families to encounter this, and our lack of understanding cannot be hidden any longer. Many churches and Christians really haven't taken the time to relate with God honestly over this topic.

If they had, my story of freedom would be a dime a dozen.

For those who share the fear I lived with for so long, who share my values, and want to find their life in the plan they believe God originally laid out for them at their creation as a man or woman, I share my story. I offer my perspectives in hope that your victory will be easier won than mine.

The Grid of Response

The conversation about homosexuality in the Church and in culture can be confusing and hard to understand. For example, it is mind-blowing to many when they hear some Christians say that the Bible doesn't actually forbid same-sex relationships. It seems very clear and the concepts behind "gay theology" are an affront to them and their reverence for the Bible. (Gay theology is a system of belief that upholds a concept of biblical justification for monogamous same-sex relationships through the use of the six primary verses in the Bible which address homosexuality.) To others, it is equally disconcerting when gay Christians are faced with careless, rhetorical asides to sermons about "Adam and Steve." (Gay Christians have defined themselves as people who have a relationship with God but have tried and failed, or don't believe they can/should change their sexual orientation. Sometimes they choose celibacy; others are sexually active in monogamous committed relationships.) Needless to say, it has become an all-out war, and it's hard for anyone to really understand what's going on from a holistic perspective when we stay bent on the idea that

---

everyone should just see it the way we do.

In an attempt to offer a little clarity (in a very non-scholarly way), I am going to share what I see from my experience on both sides of the issue.

There are basically three premises at work in this cultural debate over homosexuality. When someone encounters the issue personally from an informed Christian background, these premises are found to be at odds. This results in three primary conclusions in which one will premise must be nullified to achieve internal peace.

The premises are:

1. **God is good.**

2. **There are six primary scriptures in the Bible that address homosexuality which are traditionally interpreted to forbid it.**

3. **Some people are gay, and it's not clear if everyone can change that, but some people have.**

Obviously if you are personally or directly affected by at least two of these conditions, as a growing number of people are, then all three come into play in your life and require reconciliation. This usually yields one of three primary conclusions, or views on homosexuality, in which one premise must bow to the others:

1. **The first conclusion deals with the premise of God's goodness, and can be stated:**

"God is not good, because these scriptures forbid homosexuality, but he made people who are gay, and that is cruel."

2. **The second conclusion deals with the premise of biblical interpretation, and is summarized:**

"God is good, but the Bible is fallible and culturally relative because people are gay and they can't change."

3. **The third conclusion deals with the premise of people's ability to change, and states:**

"God is good, the Bible clearly forbids homosexuality, and people can and have changed because in His goodness God gave us power over our created bodies."

Mixtures of these primary conclusions create secondary and tertiary views that flow from these three premises. For example, some might say, *"God is good, but the Bible is fallible and culturally relative, and while some people have changed, that doesn't mean everyone can."* This is a secondary conclusion that allows for some proof from testimonies of people who have changed, while placing emphasis on the assertion that the Bible leaves its position on homosexuality open for interpretation. Countless conclusions can flow from various views and interpretations, but my aim here is just to give you the three premises that are primarily in play. You'll see all kinds of derivatives.

I personally held to the third conclusion that people should be the ones to bend and change when these premises came into conflict in my life. For the entirety of my struggle I believed I could change. I was unwavering in my adamant belief that God is good, and the Bible is trustworthy and right in its most apparent meaning. For me, it seemed the complexity of gay theology was working too hard to read between the lines in search of cultural relativism. It appeared to me to be a quest for personal justification, and looked for hidden meaning in words while the plain meaning was right there in black and white. I was mindful that the remaining body of Scripture spoke to the fact that mankind faces all kinds of challenges in his sinful nature. In the entire scope of Scripture, as far as I can see, God never seems to make exceptions in favor of the positive for anything generally referred to in the negative where holiness is concerned.

Gay theology, for example, points to the existence of slavery in Scripture and forms the premise that since we have evolved as a culture and no longer hold slaves, we should evolve on the issue of homosexual morality also. The logic always fell apart for me though, because the Bible speaks to treating a slave well, but doesn't command you to have slaves. If you don't own slaves (yay you!), then the verses offered in protection of slaves simply don't apply. Slavery is a human relational dynamic that fell away. In the Bible, acknowledgment of a cultural condition in human relations is not necessarily affirmation of it. Homosexuality then, if it follows the pattern, wouldn't then be affirmed at a later time with the evolution of culture, it would be a practice that is abandoned.

The issue of women speaking in church is another focal point used as a component of the reasoning behind gay theology. Without bogging down too much, I will simply say for now those were letters written to a specific church because of a specific problem, and not directed at the entire gender for all time. Otherwise, the female apostles and prophetesses the New Testament mentions and affirms as examples to follow would be out of line with God's order. They were clearly affirmed as valid office holders in Church government, one of them being called "outstanding among the apostles," by the same Paul who wrote the letters against women speaking up specifically in the Ephesian and Corinthian churches. It's important to see that sometimes letters are written to specific, isolated issues when viewed in the greater context of Scripture. In short, these and a lot of other reasons are why gay theology never hit the spot for me, and why I could not justify a decision to remain in homosexuality with a clear conscience based on its reasoning. It was too big of a leap for me to risk my heart's connection to the voice of God on the hope of gay theology's rickety logic.

Here's how I looked at the big picture. In general, regarding all sin, the overall narrative of the Bible tells the story that we were first created in the image of God and in full fellowship with Him — until the fall in the garden when mankind was first deceived about God's goodness and intentions toward man. Mankind from then on fell into a state of unrighteousness, which is simply defined as a distorted view of God. Since then, God has been offering redemption and restoration back to His original intent through offering man a means of righteousness — seeing God properly. I see in Genesis that His intent in the creation of mankind is for the mutual joy of God and man through unbroken fellowship and the pleasures of living life inside the bountiful and fulfilling design of God. He worked reconciliation first through the law (righteousness through works) in the Old Covenant, and then by salvation through Jesus (righteousness through faith) in the New Covenant. Most Christians agree that Jesus came not to abolish the law but to bring the fullness of it and to set forth the modern covenant of grace we live in. Through that covenant of grace we are counted righteous and — here's the fulfillment part — given power to act like it. The new covenant is entered into by faith, but that covenant also states that faith without work is dead. We're shown all throughout the New Testament that we are now empowered (and expected) to bring our old nature, inherited from the fall in the garden, into alignment with righteousness according to the grace that is available to us. This is how God restores us to His image and induces the intimate and fulfilling fellowship with Him we were created for. The process of personal redemption involves suffering, but it is also joy and brings communion and conversation with God that we innately long for. The Bible is clear all over the New Testament that we have a part to play in this act of self-transformation. It's not a passive process. Paul, for example, spoke of beating his body into submission. Or Hebrews 12:4, for example, always stood out to me with its stark boldness: *"You have not yet resisted sin to the point of shedding blood."* Those things sound odd and strange to our ears, and they may be overstated for dramatic effect, but I have to believe the point gets made. From what I discerned all during my journey, I saw that while I was already justified by faith through extravagant grace, I was also expected to wrestle against my old nature and overcome my homosexuality by the Spirit of God.

In our post-modern culture we like to look at things as if everything has layers. Complexity is admired over and above simplicity. Facebook even has "it's complicated" as a relationship status. And sometimes things *are* complex. There is some merit to that. The Barna Group and David Kinnamin have begun the conversation on how the Church can address a millennial generation with books like *unChristian* and *You Lost Me*. Based on extensive research, this conversation is helping church leaders learn how to construct a dialogue with spiritual nomads, exiles, and prodigals to build a church they will come back to. The Barna Group's message is that we need to acknowledge cultural complexity while actively keeping the gospel as simple as possible. Kinnamin and the Barna Group use Daniel as the model for maintaining faith while being fully engaged in culture. This resonates with me because all throughout my struggle, which was wrought with complex internal dialogue, I could still see the simple, identity-grounding theme of self-control in the context of grace unfolding through the entirety of Scripture's narrative. I saw the truth as simple: God is good, I'm a sinner, He gave me a way to reconciliation. I always felt it was humans who add the complexity by our desires and by the influence of our crazy culture. I was of the persuasion that the simplicity of Scripture was to lend simplicity to my life, not the other way around, with the complexity of my emotions and sexuality bringing complexity to Scripture. My belief has always been that in Scripture, as in life, the simplest and most obvious interpretation is usually the truest. The Spirit of the law is easy to discern, and excuses feel like excuses, when we get really honest.

All of that is my perspective. It's what held me on my path to freedom. Not everyone has or will reach those same conclusions, and it took me a long time to get there. At times I threw in the towel for a few bad weeks when the process of transformation was especially arduous. It didn't matter. God was faithful and patient, and He completed the good work He started in me. So while it's easy to read those words and say "yeah, that!" if you happen to agree with me, not everyone is ready to align with all that. I'm aware of that, and I'm OK with that. I share my personal view of Scripture as part of my story aimed to give hope to those who want to change. Those views held my feet on the ground, and they were life to me.

The key question of our time is learning how to respond in love when people don't agree, without compromising our view. That is where our ability to hold cultural dialogue on this issue has come to a grinding halt. We're all scratching our heads over this question. We don't know how to have this conversation. It's my belief that because the primary charge the Church receives in Scripture is to love, it's going to be our responsibility to learn how to speak about complex issues with gentleness and grace. Someone has to be the first to stop throwing punches. We can't expect those who don't hold themselves to scriptural standards to restrain their anger, venom, or agendas. So we're going to have to learn how to speak into the midst of the chaos and attract real relationship. Right now, we have a hard time with that.

Let me be really clear: I love the Church. I'm called to the Church. I'm not going anywhere. And I'm disappointed, but I'm not angry with the Church over the lack of widespread understanding. We've let some good time go to waste when we could have pressed into this issue for grace-filled responses, but until now, most people were not affected by more than one of the aforementioned realities. When that's the case, it's easy to ignore the conversation altogether. But now that we are in it, and we aren't getting out of it anytime soon, I am out to help change the conversation we *are* having because it's not working. I have great hope and vision to see a new Church who is wise as a serpent and innocent as a dove so she can be productive for harvest in this very ripe field of broken hearts. There's a reason I'm writing to the Church and to families before I write my full story for the seekers of freedom.

Since I've been discussing this topic in public, I've received a lot of anecdotal evidence regarding the state of the Church in the form of comments on my articles and blog posts. As far as I can tell, except for the churches who haven't yet been forced to respond to the issue by circumstances and relationships, most churches you might wander into on a Sunday morning fall into one of the following two camps. These camps are formed based on their acceptance of the second or third primary conclusions I described before. (Normally churches wouldn't form around the first conclusion that God is not good, but maybe they're out there!)

One portion of the Church upholds the second view — that is, that homosexuality is scripturally acceptable based on the cultural relevance of contextual verses. Out of a sense of mercy, they maintain that since some people say homosexuality is for them personally unchangeable, it must be so for all people. They argue that times have changed, and since some practices have been abandoned, the banning of homosexuality should be abandoned as well. Their view of the Bible is that it's a living document, written by flawed people who were spokespersons for their culture, but that our hearts and minds should dictate to us what is acceptable as a greater authority than Scripture. Tragically, this denies the seekers — those with a deeply held conviction that their homosexuality is wrong — any avenue of hope. They won't likely find a support system in these churches if they decide to fight their desires. These churches tend to strongly advocate politically on behalf of gay rights issues, are proponents of gay theology, and even sometimes ordain gay clergy. To be fair, their passion is for acceptance and honoring people of all kinds, and that in itself is a good and beautiful thing.

The other portion of the Church upholds the third view — they believe that God is good and gives us grace, affirm traditional biblical beliefs that homosexuality is forbidden, and believe that people can change through empowerment from the Holy Spirit. From there... unfortunately... we break down further into two different camps. My vision is to see that gap closed.

The ones who uphold the view that people can change and also see it happen in the lives around them make it a point to give room for process and let people take their time. Their view is that as long as there is an active relationship with God underway, God will speak to it and complete what He starts. I'm hopeful about the fact that many churches are beginning to have productive conversations and are becoming very well aware that this sin is like all others — a person facing it is to be treated with compassion and grace and given room to grow. Many of my own mentors walk tall in this revelation, thus my freedom and my continued ability to maintain my call to the Church are a reality to this day. One of my other favorite examples is Gateway Church in Austin, Texas. In August of 2009 they held a very eye-opening, productive church-wide Sunday morning session about the process of freedom some of their own members had been involved in. You can find the video of this service on Vimeo (http://vimeo.com/6344577). The testimony of each of these church members was that the people of Gateway loved them and gave them room to be in process. They didn't directly confront their sin any more than we directly confront someone who overeats or mishandles their money. They just loved them like everyone else — often as they brought their partners to church with them — and in that place created by love, God's voice broke into their worlds and they changed. There are other places having this conversation in productive ways as well. The Marin Foundation out of Boystown, Chicago, has also been fostering a conversation for over a decade between the Christian and LGBT cultures. They believe in a life of submersion — surrounding themselves with people in this well-known gay neighborhood to live out the love of God in a manifest and tangible way among them. I admire them for their courage to focus so much on one area of need in our culture and change people's hearts about the Church.

Sadly, though, many churches who would affirm the third view that people can change also display a sense of what they feel is righteous anger toward people they think are in rebellion. This section of the Church is often reactive and quick-fused when it comes to this topic. When someone from their own ranks admits a problem, you witness scenarios where they would seek to bring immediate change, require public apologies, and solicit solemn promises of never falling again. If the process takes too long or the switch doesn't flip once the leadership confronts the sin, they depose the fallen leader and often cast their members out of fellowship. They are often most interested in their ministry's image or Christianity's image as being intolerant of sin. Out of that, they miss an opportunity to bring about the full restoration of a heart by taking their time and seeking to understand what caused the failure. This completely denies the person a process of inward restoration and outward regulations serve to make everyone except the fallen and the struggling feel better. As a byproduct, other members who may face similar issues learn that the best thing to do with their own problem is to hide it or leave. These churches preach "every sin is the same," but I wonder what would happen if they cracked down on the other sins the Bible references as abominations as swiftly as homosexuality. Proverbs 6:16-19 references haughty eyes, lying tongues, hands that shed innocent blood, hearts that devise wicked schemes, feet that are quick to rush into evil, false witnesses who pour out lies, and a person who stirs up conflict in the community as abominations. That levels the playing field quite a bit!

As far as the greater role in culture is concerned, inside the church house, this portion of the Church usually preaches about issues like gay marriage from a defensive posture. This is normally out of a sense of duty to protect the Bible and stand up for what is right.

I understand where this comes from. I've been there myself. This approach is usually earnest and based out of a truly righteous desire to see a nation honor God with its laws and standards of morality. I believe, as Christians, we are supposed to seek that for our nation — for all nations. Many in this portion of the Church have been around when threats to normalcy such as gay marriage weren't raising their heads, and it's more than a little bit scary for them. They are serious about fulfilling the mandate Jesus left us with to disciple nations, and they want to be faithful to the call.

Outside its walls, when this portion of the Church is engaging culture, the mission to disciple the nation tends to break down quickly. Rather than forming understanding and honest relationships on a personal level with people in the gay community, we engage the hierarchy of that community in political battles and culture wars. I submit that the swift and decisive approach taken with its own fallen members is derived from the same source that drives some of the Church to attempt to contain this issue in our culture primarily by means of legislation. That source is fear of relationship, and if it's not fear, it's lack of desire to do the hard work required by relationship. The political system was never intended to be a means of discipleship. Promoting legislation that bandages the problem actually concedes to civil rulers the authority to govern morality. Honestly, it seems like the easy way out. A diminished prevalence of homosexuality in our culture by means of legislation would not only be a façade, if somehow achieved, but also inconsistent with how Jesus modeled cultural redemption and transformation.

Jesus spoke of a Kingdom that was not of this earth, and told us to bring people into it. Much of this portion of the Church cries out for a returning to our roots as a Christian nation, but it seems to me that if the hearts we are called to disciple are still unrighteous, we're still not a Christian nation — no matter how we managed to get our laws passed and leaders elected. I further propose to you that we could have 100% Christian leadership in office, and 100% of the laws on our books could align with biblical worldview, and we could still be deemed a "goat nation." Jesus spoke of those who followed the law but had dark hearts as being "whitewashed tombs." This is what we'll achieve for our nation if we don't tend to the hearts in our garden. The hope and beauty of the American system is that if we as the Church were to stop being afraid and do the hard work of relationship-based discipleship, the laws and officeholders who govern us would eventually reflect what we fight tooth and nail for in every election cycle.

Since we *are* having to fight so hard, I maintain we have not done due diligence to relate to this portion of our culture with honor and winsome speech. For a long time now, we have been talking about gay issues and announcing that homosexuality is a sin, which many like to think is "speaking forth the truth in love," but if this portion of the Church truly believes people can change, then somehow we're failing at creating the environment where people feel safe enough for this to happen.

The problem is this: The loudest, clearest, and sometimes only message the Church is sending into the culture right now about homosexuality is that it's an abomination and our political message that we're against gay marriage. While it's necessary for Christians to take part in the American political process, we have our citizenship first in the Kingdom of God and the primary responsibility we have is to give the *good* news. We have American rights and should use them wisely, but our American rights are secondary to our Christian privileges and responsibilities. Discipling nations starts with hearts. We have to be saying more, and our message of hope and unconditional love should not be a byline on our political talking points — it should be the main thing people hear. *Until we change this*, enemies will continue to be made of flesh-and-blood human faces, and the Church will continue to lose her potential to touch the hearts of the individuals all around them because they're witnessing the sad, miserable process.

With this framework on the culture's and Church's various positions in place, let me bring us back to the discussion of the three primary conclusions people draw from the three premises that are at war (God is good, the Bible forbids homosexuality, people are gay). I've illustrated that this is where the dividing lines are in the culture and Church, and it seems obvious this is where most families break down. I want to offer some ideas on how to have a conversation and keep the peace when these ideologies are at war in a home and threaten to divide a family. People can easily vacillate between these conclusions, but it seems to me most hold one of them as a primary persuasion when looking at the three premises we're talking about.

Say your family member is stuck on the first conclusion, that God is a cruel being who created an innate problem in mankind and then condemned him to hell for his sin. The lie working against them is that God is cruel. As we know, every believable lie contains elements of truth. The portion of truth in their greater struggle is they are acknowledging *some authority* in the Bible. If Christians quoting the Bible at them or the verses that speak to homosexuality are the reason they are angry at God, then the Bible clearly has merit with them. The approach you want to take then is to use the strength of the Bible to affirm God's goodness. You're looking to secure them, and since they have placed a certain merit on the Word, use their strength *for* them. Find places in the Word that express the love of God. Emphasize the grace of God, the beauty of the plan of redemption and the great sacrifice God made because of His love for us. Go on a hunt for all the passages that will highlight nothing but the love of God to them. It may surprise them at first, and they may quote passages back at you where God devastated an enemy camp or flooded the earth. Instead of defending that, acknowledge that Scripture does have complex moments, but don't argue theology. Don't allow yourself to get into dogmatic battles over stories; just point out to them that there is proof in Scripture that God created them with purpose and loves them deeply. If it's more than dogma to them and they want to go deeper and study out the difficult passages, be prepared to do that. Every young generation wants someone to dive deep and face the challenges with them. Your willingness to do that without an argumentative spirit, but with a humble open heart will speak volumes to them. Live that out. Unconditionally. For as long as it takes. God is not angry with them, and He's not out to punish them. So mirror that. Also, when you discover stories of people who have been able to change their sexual orientation, relay those stories to them. Be sensitive to timing and tone, but try to find a way to share it. You want to do this carefully — your aim is to relieve the pressure of the lie they're believing — that God is evil because He made a rule against something people can't change. If you show them that people have been able to access His grace and His love and *have changed*, the pressure-packed belief starts to lose steam. Again, the goal is not to argue, but to reconcile two opposing view points. There is already a war in their mind, so don't add your guns to it. The Spirit will lead you if you stay at peace.

In another scenario, a loved one might be more stuck on the second view, that since God is good and people can't change, the Bible must be flawed. I know I'm stating the obvious, but in this case, it's not going to be wise to use Scripture to convince them the Bible isn't flawed. Your loved one already believes God is good. You'll want to emphasize stories of redemption and transformation, where the principles of Scripture have been successfully and joyfully implemented. Highlight testimonies that speak to God's ability to move a person from a helpless, impossible state to overcome their odds and be made new. Use their belief in the goodness of God as a springboard into discussions and stories about the power of the resurrection that afforded humanity the power to be victorious over anything that seeks to defeat us. Also helpful, when I have had times of doubting Scripture, authors like C.S. Lewis have bolstered my faith from a logical standpoint and landed me back in love with Scripture. You might see if any of his works speak to your family's situation.

Of course, if your loved one is of the third persuasion that God is good, the Bible is inerrant, and people can change, then just offer them patience and a shoulder to cry on when the battle gets fiery and the nights get long. They face pressure from all sides in culture to quit fighting and come out. Don't add to the pressure by assigning due dates to their freedom. Setbacks may (and probably will) come, and your response will be pivotal to their courage to keep fighting. God will completely work in anyone who stands there long enough demanding it by faith.

The bottom line is this: Love covers a multitude of sins. Perfect love drives out fear. Humility doesn't threaten. Honor seeks a person's strengths and secures them by allowing them room to operate out of their strengths. Love avoids picking at weaknesses to win a battle. Winsome conversation avoids the point of contention and dialogues from a place of common ground. We have to move to this posture if the gospel will be successful in this community.

So I'm calling for new voices.

We need voices who lead us in a new approach to this topic that gets the job done. We need them to inspire belief that people can change if they want to. We need them to bravely confront old mindsets and relational approaches that don't work. We need them to take the risk and form the tension between grace for process and the unchanging standards of holy behavior set forth in Scripture. We need them to create the place where perfect love drives out fear, where evil is overcome by good, where with our faith we please God, and where great hope gives birth to unlikely freedom. I consider it to be the responsibility of people like myself and my parents, who have been inside this struggle and inside these churches, to stir up this new level of conversation. Our singular goal is to be offering this hope to the hopeless, this drink to the thirsty. We, the Church, are called to equip the saints and reconcile the unregenerate soul back to God, and it is clear, from the din of our unproductive culture wars, that it has never been more essential and timely that we find our Savior's voice on this topic.

In God's economy, our struggles are never wasted. Parents, families, and friends who walk this road with their loved ones will be the new voices who rise up to offer redemption and freedom to an entire generation. Without these wounded healers, a generation may never know what it means to experience the unconditional love of God and the source of joy and life that fellowship with God's people can be when peace reigns supreme.

Won't People Be Hurt By This Message?

I know this is not a politically correct message.

I recognize my voice is smaller than pop-culture and the media, smaller than theological institutions who have found scholarly-sounding answers that placate the culture.

I realize I'm up against a giant that's constantly feeding the idea that homosexuality is en vogue, even to those who aren't gay.

I know many are offended by the concept that homosexuality can be a choice.

I know many people would say it's dangerous and irresponsible to advocate that a person can change their sexual preference because of so many who have been hopeless and wounded in the fight.

I know we have lost so many dear, precious people to suicide over this very struggle. I was nearly one of them. More than once.

And as much as I know the pain of this struggle, I also know that this is not the unforgivable sin, and that God does not demand immediate victory.

He is a patient, long-suffering Father who would rather us live with purpose and bear up under some struggle than abandon life altogether.

I know a lot of people will disagree with the premise of my writing and would like to discount my story. They may say I was never gay. Or that I'm still gay.

To that I ask, "Why would I write this headache upon myself?"

Further, I would lovingly beg of you not to hang your heart on the fragile assumption that my story and stories like mine are false (and that change isn't possible). The condition of your heart is the only thing you take with you when you leave this life — and it's a lot to risk.

Let me comfort you by saying I know some day I will answer to God for any empty words I speak or write.

"But I tell you that everyone will have to give account on the day of judgment for every empty word they have spoken. For by your words you will be acquitted, and by your words you will be condemned." — Jesus, Matthew 12:36, 37

I assure you, these pages are not filled with such words.

I have close, amazing friends in the LGBT community. I love them and I maintain that they have the free will and God-given right to pursue the life they desire. My heart always loves, honors, and believes the best for them. I pray I can speak from my story in a way that both honors and challenges them, and builds stronger bridges between us.

Honestly, I'd like to apologize both to the people I know personally, and to the LGBT community as a whole, for the irresponsible way many Christians have handled their relationship to the community. In large part, we've responded in fear. We've been prideful. We've acted like we are much cleaner, holier people. In many cases, we've tried to be your Holy Spirit. We've tried to persuade you of your unrighteousness by our own doctrinal lectures and poured out our own brand of conviction so you would be afraid enough to be repentant. We've not stopped to understand. We've not asked questions. We've just assumed a lot of things about your goodness as a person. And, really, when we've failed to do that and spoken out of theory and relational ignorance, we've gotten in the way of a process God may have already had you in. We've done everything but love your hearts as Christ would. Not all Christians, but far too many.

It's been horrendously painful and grieving to watch, as someone who understands where both sides are coming from. All I can say is, I'm truly, deeply, sorry. And, as I did in the previous chapter, I've tried to speak to the Christian community when things get out of hand, and ask them to consider the methods and reasons by which they speak out on cultural levels. I've advocated for lowering the guns in the culture war. The good news is, I'm not the only one saying it, and some people are listening. Not everyone, but some.

What I'm sharing here is not more of the same heated rhetoric. I'm endeavoring to start a new conversation that is less concerned with your civil rights to marry or not marry, and more concerned with the spiritual condition of your heart.

Setting my fear of controversy aside and acknowledging with sadness the potential of losing valuable friendships in the LGBT community, what I can't forget is that in my heart, even as a young girl, I had an internally originating conviction that the way I felt toward women was not God's best for me.

I cannot help but believe there are others who, like I did, feel unwanted homosexual desire that goes against their will and convictions.

And so I am compelled by love to speak. To them. For them. For hope.

I can't pretend to have all the answers. The chasm between the gay and straight communities is widening in some parts and coming together in other parts of our society. In my opinion, it needs to come a lot closer together, and it only stays apart because of fear.

The greatest tragedy of all exists when the chasm between communities splits a family, and all parties involved find it non-traversable. Separation from the love of our families is second in torment only to separation from the love of God. There is a reason suicide among homosexual teens is so high, and that ad campaigns like Dan Savage's "It Gets Better" have come into existence.

The important thing is that we always love and that we commit to a long-term attempt to understand each other. We can't be afraid to give audible words to the conversation that's already happening in our hearts. We can't let the lies change the faces of our loved ones into strangers. We can't be offended by honesty and questions.

I believe love is primarily a decision, and it's nice when it's backed up by feelings, but that's not always a luxury we have. When this issue arises to challenge a family, it's more important than ever to stick to that decision, no matter where our feelings take us. We must offer solutions that work. Solutions that build people up and empower them to make choices — out of their own volition — that are healthy. We must offer power, hope, patience, strength, resilience... to those who have decided they want to be straight and are struggling to get there.

I tell my story because so many people are afraid to tell this story for themselves — of a straight person, who struggled to stay straight, because they saw being straight as a thing of value and honor.

How to Have this Conversation

The thing we, as Christians, in telling our stories and our truths have to remember is this: We must seek to honor all men, including those who disagree with us. 1 Peter 2:17 (NKJV): *"Honor all people. Love the brotherhood. Fear God. Honor the king."*

Let me emphasize that: We must honor ALL people.

"I urge, then, first of all, that petitions, prayers, intercession and thanksgiving be made for all people — for kings and all those in authority, that we may live peaceful and quiet lives in all godliness and holiness. This is good, and pleases God our Savior, who wants all people to be saved and to come to a knowledge of the truth." — The Apostle Paul, 1 Timothy 2:1-4

We are *required* to give thanks for *all* people. Let that sink in.

Now, while we are undeniably bound by this call to a magnitude of love and honor that surpasses human ability and places demand on the better angels of our nature, we also have to remember that the Holy Spirit is still quietly and faithfully doing His job. He's always preparing *someone's* heart for another step closer into friendship with God by addressing issues of their identity. We must be unafraid to open our mouths and share our portion of the light.

Lies exist, and they grow tall and strong in the fertile ground of un-illuminated hearts. We all have areas in our spirits that are not yet illuminated, but some parts *have* been given light, and from that light, we are responsible to speak. To withhold truth from a person in need is ultimately dishonoring.

So, in the context of honor, we speak the truth. If we are compelled by love, our message will be in timing and will carry both honor *and* truth.

While the resistance to truth flows loud and strong, and sometimes dishonorably, from those who do not see right and wrong through traditional biblical interpretations on homosexuality, we cannot become ensnared by that and fall into arguments and unproductive conversations. Again, all people have the right to pursue their own desired lives, but some people desire a life that lies in opposition to the homosexual feelings they experience. To those, we are called.

No matter how strong the cultural tide of any particular bent away from Christ is, we cannot forget there is a God-given cry on the inside of the majority of people to know and live in truth.

We can and must be respectful and responsible with our truths at all times, but we cannot always save the ears of those who disagree. Because our calling is to those who hunger for inward peace with God, to those who are seeking solace for their souls, we must unapologetically blanket the culture with hope in search of them. While the enemy uses culture to shame them into silence, we must speak up and offer shelter. We must spread the good news that in His presence there is peace, reconciliation, and love. We must tell them they have options, and one option is to allow God permission to transform their lives.

It's OK To Fight.

All of my discussion on Church and culture to this point has been leading up to this section. This is the message I hope to see raised like a banner above all other messages the Church sends. This is the message I pray every family can adopt as their motto when a family member comes to terms with their struggle.

I believe it's the missing message in our culture today, and that is this:

It's *OK* to fight, if you don't want to feel same-sex attraction. You *can* overcome it. And if you choose to fight, you deserve a pressure-free process.

There is honor in fighting, and there is a place for your voice in society if you choose not to embrace homosexuality for yourself.

There is honor in desiring to desire someone of the opposite sex (yes, sexually), even if you don't desire that today.

There is honor in embracing the natural process of procreation and adhering to the originally intended functions of your sexual organs and reproductive system.

There is honor in embracing God's choice of your gender, and choosing not to alter yourself.

It's OK to honor God. In this way. With these things. And someone needs to say so.

Our culture has managed to script our perspectives for us. We have all come to understand, according to pop culture and the media, that being straight means you are boring, uncreative, and living in a religious box. Being straight and completely supportive of homosexuality with no questions asked means you are hip, enlightened, and on the societal high ground.

We have to quit believing that, and quit belittling people on *both* sides of this issue.

This tainting of our vision is as old (and immature) as the lunchtime seating dilemma faced by the nerds and popular kids in junior high cafeterias everywhere.

It needs to stop.

I recognize that all who experience same-sex attraction are not compelled to change in the way that I was. I honor you, seek friendship with you, and I do not judge you. It's not my job to change you or convict you to change — that is God's business. It's my job to love and honor you. Your life is valuable and God is very capable of speaking to your heart when and if your time comes to fight this battle.

I acknowledge that maybe some haven't been called to fight their homosexuality or same-sex attraction yet. Maybe they won't ever hear God's whisper in their heart saying, "It's your time to fight."

But, there are those who do not want that life.

Some of them are young and no one is telling them it's OK to fight. Culture only tells them "it gets better." To get comfortable with their uncomfortableness, but maybe they don't want that. Maybe, like me, on the inside, away from anyone else's influence or voice on the matter, they want to change. They are a boy or young man, currently attracted to other young men, but they want to become a man who dates and marries a woman. Or, they are a girl or young lady currently attracted to other young ladies, but they want to become a woman who dates and marries a man. I know they are out there. I know them. I *was* them.

Who is speaking for *them*? Who is giving *them* hope?

As I have been doing, let me again interject here: I think it's a shame how some Christians treat the LGBT community. If they are the lepers, we are the Pharisees. In many cases. *Far* too many. It is horrendous and tragic, and it *is* unenlightened.

But the contented individual who is happy in homosexuality is not the audience this message is directed toward.

And I know there is room for more than one message in our culture.

As needed and valuable as campaigns to stop teenage suicide are in the LGBT community, equally important is the message that there is hope for you if you don't want to experience homosexual, or bisexual, or transgender feelings. You can be free to live in the body God gave you, just like it is, and express your sexuality just as God designed — both for pleasure and for procreation. Offering this hope along with the relational support to substantiate it through changing the message the culture is hearing is another life-affirming way to look at homosexuality. This message, too, can prevent suicide.

Parents can be a base of strength in bringing this message to the culture. Friends and families of the LGBT community don't have to take a weak stance of denying principles they have raised their children with, and they don't have to take a posture of fear and defensiveness either. We can create the tension between mercy and judgment, which is love and truth — a tension that boldly declares "it's OK to fight." The resistance to this message would say "I have gay friends, or I have a gay child, and they can't change. Do you think God made a mistake with them? Do you think they are less valuable as people?" That's not the question we are answering. The question we are answering is, "If I don't want to be gay, is there hope for me?"

The answer is yes. Resoundingly, *yes*. The people asking this question deserve an advocate. They deserve hope. They deserve a community of people who will stand with them until they can see God.

FAMILY

To Parents

In my freedom years, my parents and I have discussed our journey in times of intentional healing and reflection. It was awkward, but it was necessary to bring full restoration of relationship. You don't go through a thing like that together, and then pretend it never happened. As I emerged into freedom, I moved from a self-focused, survival-based position in life to a place where I sought to understand the impact it had on them, for my own closure and for theirs. During the course of these discussions, there is one thing I came to know: it affected all of us equally from the moment I confessed my struggles to them, maybe not in manifestation, but certainly in magnitude.

I learned that my dad struggled with depression when I left home and both my parents had to war against the weight of shame as it pressed down on their spirits to condemn them for my failures and confusion. They had to fight against internal lies telling them they raised me wrong. They took upon themselves quite a cross, and they indeed followed Him. And they mostly did it alone.

They were careful never to let me in on this pain in great detail while I was still fighting for my life in my own ways. Learning later what I could never have handled knowing then brought to me an altogether different kind of grief and horror than I'd ever experienced.

I share this because I want to speak to parents, family members, and friends who can relate to what my parents went through. I want to tell you I'm so sorry for how you're hurting. As someone who has wrestled with this haunting lie, I can assure you that the pain you feel is something that is most likely inaccessible to the perceptions of your loved one, even if you've told them how it hurts. There is even an element in what they are going through that would cause them to be angered by your pain, which certainly only adds to your sorrow. Concern for you is almost an unattainable place of compassion or awareness for them right now, but it does not discount the validity of the pain you are feeling. Your anguish comes from love, and it is an honorable burden you bear.

I pray you will someday rejoice with your loved one as I did with my parents. It brought me great joy to know that the torment they experienced had been brought to an end when I emerged victorious from my fight.

Until that day, you still have to tend your own soul as you pray for your loved one. It is so easy to be catapulted by a range of emotions into unproductive, unhealthy, and self-defeating cycles of relationship when we come to a place of grief like this. I offer these next few chapters in hope to steady you with honor, truth, and compassion for your time of need.

———

At the risk of sounding trite, let's reflect on the fact that God the Father watched His Son take upon Himself all the sin of the world. Jesus bore the wrath of His Father and the condemnation for this very sin in order to redeem us. Because of this, there is a Father who has watched His Son bear up under the weight of this exact spiritual war. Take your comfort in the Father's heart, and He will teach you how He survived this. I can see that God had to place faith in His Son's decisions and trust Jesus to carry out His will. I'm not a parent, but I can't imagine the scenario felt a lot different from what you might be feeling as you trust your son or daughter to work out their faith on this issue.

Nothing seems more appropriate right now than a letter from my parents, so that you know you are not alone. This was originally written to some friends of my parents who went through this with their son. They wrote it to them just a short time after their son broke the news of his struggle with same-sex attraction. It covers so many bases of what you may be going through, so I think it's beneficial to include it for you.

A Letter From My Parents

Dear _____ and _____,

Sharon and I are reminded of our experiences with Christy and all the emotions that ran through our lives during this time. It was very painful for us and I'm certain it is very painful for you as well. Let me assure you that God is your source of strength and HE will love you through this just as you will need to love your precious son through this, too. Christy has better insight than we do into what he is going through, but we can tell you our part of the story. Looking back, the best thing we did for Christy (and us) was to communicate to her that we did not have all the answers about steps forward. We knew what we believed, and most importantly, we knew our love would never change for her. We told her we intended to love her through this as well. She was surrounded by people who gently cared for her, provided an environment where she could not be pressured, but would have the opportunity to reflect on the impact of her directions. We prayed — everyone we could share with prayed. Christy had "the spiritual base," that I'm sure your son has — that [base] she used to sort this out and make good decisions with the loving help of God and others He placed in her life.

Please know that Sharon and I are all too aware of what questions and emotions are flowing through your minds, as parents, during this time: extreme guilt, grief (like the loss of a loved one), anger, shame, hopelessness, helplessness, and fear — everything, including the feeling that nothing will ever be the same. It is the perfect storm in which Satan has an excellent opportunity to destroy the entire family — if the family allows it. God provides inexplicable strength during this time to help you get your head off your pillow, go to the office and do your job, and be who you need to be for others — only Him. Your child is constantly on your mind, even when you are dealing with life — because of your love for him. Turn these thoughts into prayers for him as much as you can — not distress. This is a spiritual battle that requires strength and determination to pull together, exercise a seemingly irrational faith in Him that He not only has your backside, but all sides in this battle, and He is stronger than the lies your son is being fed. Reclaim your son spiritually before God.

Time has helped me understand that it is not so much about the background of the individual as it is about how many of the lies the individual takes in and believes from the evil one that distorts their view of themselves and who they are in God. This is something that I believe will become clearer to you as you move through this.

Finally, Sharon and I did not have the benefit of being able to share with anyone what we were going through or being able to talk to anyone about similar experiences. I'm not sure we would have, even if given the opportunity, but I can tell you that hindsight tells me it would have helped us. We understand your need to be discreet and you have to decide what is best for you. We are praying for each of you and are certainly available to you to pray and share as you feel comfortable. We don't have all the answers — just the experience.

We also want you to know that, while this was a very difficult time in our lives, we are all now stronger as a result. Christy is restored and we are closer than ever. This experience is directly responsible for a lot of that closeness. All of our lives are restored because of Him. We don't dwell anymore on what we did wrong. We focus on what we can do right for and with Christy. We never really sorted all that out anyway and I don't think you will either. We have asked for and received forgiveness for anything that God brought to mind and are now focused on what is in front of us.

You are on our hearts and in our prayers. It is not hopeless. God is very capable of turning this around instantly if He chooses. Your faith is very important in staying on the same page with your son and between yourselves. Love, Love, Love! You will grow. Let us know how we can help.

With love,

Mike and Sharon

Grief: Yours and Theirs

"The day you left was the day the music died." These were the words my mom used to describe the day I packed up and left home in search of a new life. If you knew what music means to my Mom, this would be a clear statement of grief and devastation.

While I buried my face in my sheets for weeks on end in my new city, wrapped in blankets mid-summer and swaddled hopelessly in the sounds of sorrowful instrumental piano CD's grieving the loss of my first romantic love, I had no idea of the storm gathering in my family's hearts.

When faces change, hearts don't know what to do. The revelation that your son or daughter has embraced an entire lifestyle contrary to your upbringing, contrary to conventional interpretation of Scripture, and outside of all that seems safe, would reasonably leave you in a place of grief entirely unfamiliar to you.

It's not wrong to feel grief.

When Jesus heard of Lazarus' death and saw the grief Mary, Martha and the entire village shared, he wept. This is that verse, when "Jesus wept." That verse comes after Jesus had already shared His plans for this tragedy to end in glory. He had already announced His plans to restore Lazarus to life. Yet curiously, He still paused and genuinely grieved with the town to the point that they said, "See how He loved Lazarus. Could He not also have prevented his death?"

Because of Jesus' compassionate example, we can be comforted in the fact that there is no dichotomy in having faith strong enough to raise the dead, but also experiencing very real grief. Our mourning is natural. It expresses value for the one whom we lament. Grief expresses regret for their loss and our sense of disconnection, however temporary it may be.

In your grief as a parent, it may be of comfort to you that your loved one is probably also grieving. This would be particularly true if they have chosen to leave a partner in pursuit of their desire for freedom. No matter how wrong they themselves may feel the ended relationship was, they are still invested in this person and will experience a very real loss when they terminate the connection. It's important to understand that they are scripturally free to grieve, even as they pursue and believe for change.

Recently I had lunch with a dear brother from the U.K. He is a Christian who grew up in the underage gay clubbing scene before he encountered Christ through a gay friend who took him to church. Years later, now a seminary student, he is still waiting for his desires to change, but has committed to remaining celibate and pursuing a life in ministry. All through his journey, he was surrounded by a church family who honored the gift in him and gave him freedom to lead worship. But in order to do this, he had to break up with a man he deeply loved. Willing to make the sacrifice and not looking back at it, he still laments that his only regret for pursuing God is that he had to hurt someone he cared about to do so. Grief is a very real part of the equation in many earnest quests for freedom.

There is another grief that can be at work in a person who is fighting their homosexual desires. You may only be learning of the struggle today, but they may be weary, exhausted, and full of disappointment about the difficulty of reorientation. It is very easy to come to a place of low-grade, persistent grief and sadness over the constant inability to access a renewed identity that always seems to be slightly out of reach. I could compare it to a woman who tries for years to get pregnant, then miscarries multiple times, and never is certain whether her next pregnancy will "take." It is a life, a vision for life, and it's not as easily attained as science and biology might make it seem, at least in the pregnancy example.

A third kind of grief can be present when a person feels that they are sacrificing a large portion of who they know themselves to be in exchange for something — and Someone — still unfamiliar to them, if they are a new Christian.

Knowing the grief your loved one is experiencing is not a cure for your own grief. They are not experiencing the feelings that are unique to your role in their life, but knowing about it can be helpful. It can allow you perspective, and reduce the sting of your own sense of victimization. If you know the temptation for isolation out of grief is equally relevant to the other person, you may find in that awareness the impetus to extend unconditional love. The truth is, as a family, you are not alone on either side of the struggle, and this reality can potentially serve as a powerful connecting point for conversation and compassion toward each other. Letting each other in — asking your child or loved one about the grief they may be feeling — could be a huge key to unlocking the door to a room filled with essential, even life-saving, conversation and the kind of heart-level connectedness the enemy of your family desperately seeks to steal.

Don't Overreact

Two things: Fear and religion are your enemies. DO NOT speak from them. Shut them up, strangle them to death, quiet their foolish mouths! Cut. Out. Their. Tongues. Be violent against their fire!

Love is the answer. Speak from it. If you can't yet, then just don't speak. Seriously.

Here's why.

James 3:5-6 shows us how the entire course of our lives can be set on fire by the kind of words which arise when making demands: *"Consider what a great forest is set on fire by a small spark. The tongue also is a fire, a world of evil among the parts of the body. It corrupts the whole person, sets the whole course of his life on fire, and is itself set on fire by hell."*

While this passage in James warns us of the death our words can bring, Proverbs 18:21 promises us life : *"The tongue has the power of life and death, and those who love it will eat its fruit."* You could read this verse to say that fruit does not have to be produced for the positive or negative, if we don't speak. If we don't love the tongue — read: the sound of our own voices — we can put the fruit producing on hold until we can keep from setting our families on fire with demands.

I'm not advocating eternal silence, but if you need time to process what you're going through, just be silent for a while. It's OK to do that.

If you're reading this book as a parent who cares for their child, it's likely you are a good parent, and you love your child to the best of your abilities.

You're their strongest orientation on what love is.

Let me put it this way: From the time we are children, parents are the earth, representing all that is stable and permanent, including God our Father. A parent's unconditional love is to a kid what gravity is to earth — a mirror that reflects the permanency of God and His love, and keeps us anchored to Him. It's always there. It doesn't change. It's predictable.

Later in life, when sons and daughters board rocket ships to other universes, they load up their fuel tanks with their own good reasons to explore, and they prepare for the resistance they'll meet as their emotional outbursts serve as a countdown to the moment of liftoff. Their deceit, anger, emotional distance, and all forms of betrayal are forces working against the gravity of your love. You feel burned because this is what happens to the ground under a rocket ship. It's how it's supposed to feel. Love gets burned... because it doesn't move. It's like the earth. It's like God.

No one boards a rocket ship for another universe and expects to float away without the jet fuel. They know there is going to be some amount of resistance, so they will produce some fire and a powerful pushing away. Your job is to be the ground that doesn't move, to be the gravity the astronaut feels as the rocket leaves the earth.

If you speak out of fear, out of anger, out of pain, out of any of the things you are feeling when the burners begin firing at you, you set up a scenario where gravity lets go. The ground beneath the rocket then falls away, and all the trustworthy forces of natural law are no longer steadfast or predictable at a time when certainty from you, as the ambassador of steadfast love, is needed most.

If your love gets afraid just because your kid dons an astronaut suit and prepares for space flight, it's like the rules of nature changed and made way for the suit. This is unexpected, and it empowers the lies. As humans we're drawn to power, so a more permanent disorientation is even more likely if your loved one can see that what they are currently doing is more powerful than what they've always known to be true in relationship with you.

So don't let it be more powerful. Be the quiet, immovable earth. The one illuminated by the sun when astronauts look back from space. Speak words that hold their hearts to yours. Like you always have. Don't change.

Your son or daughter is not expecting you to embrace their decisions in a way that denies who you are and what you stand for, no matter how much they say they are. Your known standards of morality aren't supposed to change any more than gravity lets go when you get close to earth. And neither is your love for them.

At times, these standards and your love will seem to be an impossible dichotomy of contradiction. But this is God. Compelled by love, He honors, but sets forth the truth for us. Our response should mirror this. It forms a perfect tension where faith, hope, and love can do their best work.

You make your love known. You make your standards of morality quietly evident. You stand by those things, unashamedly, and reconcile that tension for them by continuing to be gravity every time they interact with you. Not by overstating it, but by loving them, and by answering honestly when they want your blessing on their new planetary residence.

"I love you, but I don't embrace this with you. It's not who you are. It's not the world you were made for."

Fear

In my parents' letter, my dad writes in reference to my struggle with homosexuality that it was an occasion in which *"Satan has an excellent opportunity to destroy the entire family — if the family allows it."*

The good news is that the family doesn't have to allow that.

Fear thrives in situations that present stark and shocking facts. It creates a fuzz of panic in which we become its slaves. It taps into our adrenal systems and can rule our decisions for hours. We learned from the third chapter of James that's all the time it needs to get a foothold on the course of entire relationships.

We're humans. We are the type of people who like to stick to our guns.

If we make demands while fear is king on the throne of our hearts, pride and its armies are tempted to back it up for a long time to come. When we respond to the things our loved ones trust us with from this place, we lock ourselves and those relationships onto a trajectory of hopelessness, division, and maybe even death.

Fear is always about self-preservation.

Fear lies to us about our motives. We see our loved ones venturing off into unfamiliar territories, and we worry for their souls. We want to do something to stop it, to save them, to keep them from danger. All this is very natural and being aware of these realities is powerful fuel for sustaining a prayer life. But, while masking itself to our own hearts as heroic protectionism or extreme love, fear almost always causes us to think about a way to override another person's will. Fear even hides itself in mercy and hospitality. We're "afraid for someone," so we do this, or do that — without their permission. We hope they take our offering or suggestion, then we get cranky and anxious and loud when they assert their own will. Then we start making demands.

There is a reason the Bible says perfect love drives out fear.

Fear brings pressure with its demands. Fear can't see another option beyond it's own very forceful solution. It seeks control. It does not trust, it does not believe the best, and it speaks before it thinks. It needs its way, and it needs it now.

Fear reserves no hope for another person to find restoration if left to their own devices, and therefore exerts its will over them on the premise of saving them, or doing what's best for them. Even when fear would set up righteous circumstances for another person which would ultimately yield a healthier environment, fear is a wrong motivator because it breaks the free will of another person.

Free will is an important component of freedom. People need their autonomy if any change they make will become their own, and therefore be enduring. This is true *especially* when we are trying to overcome sin, not *except* when sin is a factor. Our free will, as humans, is the most effective weapon God equipped us with by which we may guard our own hearts from evil. Love knows this, and love always hopes. Where fear would have us create another person's safe new world, love would have us spur another on to do so for themselves. Hebrews 10:23-24 says it this way: *"Let us hold unswervingly to the hope we profess, for He who promised is faithful. And let us consider how we may spur one another on toward love and good deeds."*

It is our own willful resistance to the devil that drives him away, not the manufactured circumstances set up by those who love us. James 4:7 tells us, *"Submit yourselves to God... Resist the devil, and he will flee from you."* It does not say, *"Let someone submit you to God... hide from the devil and let someone resist him for you."*

Obviously, in rare circumstances such as life-threatening situations, especially when minors are involved, an intervention may be necessary. This would truly be the option love would orchestrate, but this is also the nuclear option. There is always a season of mistrust after an intervention. This seasons lasts until that person comes to see your reasons for themselves, agrees with them, and aligns their own will with what you decided for them. If you seek long-term restoration instead of a temporary fix, be sure you weigh your options.

Interventions can only happen so many times before rebellion takes over. We are innately aware that we must choose righteousness for ourselves, if it is to be chosen, and someone always choosing it for us leaves us vulnerable to unrighteousness. It is very hard to make a distinction of *your* will when someone is declaring *their* will over you. Out of a need to feel empowered and take back their personhood, many people will rebel against righteousness, even when it wouldn't be their first choice.

Fear is a crafty thief; it'll take what it can, when it can, and it plays for keeps.

We must work to be wise to its ways and overcome its evil with the greater weapons God has given us: faith, hope, and love.

My dad puts it this way: "Love must become a parent's default response to all circumstances. It is the bonding agent that sustains and strengthens relationships under stress. When the 'righteous' world and our own human nature dictate a response involving anger, demands, and rejection, a parent must choose love."

Religion

For a Christian, when their child, family member, or friend walks outside the bounds of biblical morality, one of the most tempting responses is to begin quoting scriptures to urge them back inside the safety zone.

Many times this is done in love, is permitted or requested by the hearer, and the Word does its work and washes the heart. When it's successful, it's nearly always in part because it's done in the context of a trusting relationship (theological accuracy helps a great deal, too). If it's prompted by the Spirit, conversing over Scripture can be very powerful, healing, and restorative.

A lot of the time, however, it can be really counter-productive, and that happens when it's done out of either fear or religious anxiety, and outside the context of trust and permission.

Let's go back to the principle that unsolicited truth is usually only heard as criticism. It takes a great deal of emotional agility, relational skill, and depth of character to welcome and receive unexpected or unsolicited advice — even more so on a matter as intimate as sexuality.

Busting out our favorite scriptures detailing the error of our family member's or friend's way is perhaps the least effective thing we can do if we want to build trust and draw them into repentance.

Seth Godin, famous Internet marketing guru, came out with a book called *Permission Marketing* in 1999 that changed the way the business culture handled marketing. Its premise was that if you want to turn strangers into friends and friends into customers, you must earn their trust by asking their permission to talk about your product. Once you have their permission, you should have something of value prepared to say to your customer. You should always be perpetuating the permission cycle by the helpful and relevant content of your message and acknowledging their boundaries by continuing, at appropriate times, to request permission for more conversation. The publisher's book summary describes it as a "groundbreaking concept that enables marketers to shape their message so that consumers will willingly accept it... Instead of annoying potential customers... Permission Marketing offers consumers incentives to accept advertising voluntarily."

In summary, *"Permission Marketing enables companies to develop long-term relationships with customers, create trust, build brand awareness — and greatly improve the chances of making a sale."*

As a result of this line of thinking, today we have opt-out options on the bottom of emails we receive from businesses and organizations. Anyone who doesn't have an unsubscribe button seems shady and we often report their messages as spam. You may even get offended if you get another email after unsubscribing or marking them as spam. I remember emailing a man seventeen times in a two-month span to take me off his list! I continued to receive many emails from him with no acknowledgment of my request. I was hot! The point is, the more transparent a company is with their means of acquiring your information and the more control they give you over when and how they use your information, the more likely you are to listen to what they actually have to say in their email.

I don't read spam. Do you?

The permission cycle is not a marketing tactic. It's human relations common sense, and it applies to families, and Scripture, and this topic of morality.

Let's re-phrase Godin's book summary for our purposes:

"Permission Conversation enables Christians to develop long-term relationships with people they love, create trust, build message awareness -- and greatly improve the chances of positive response."

There is a reason Jesus modeled a one-by-one, interpersonal, relationship-based, intimate implementation of the good news. It works best that way.

He was the original permission marketer. He said, "Follow me," and they did. They didn't have to, but they did. By the way, they weren't Christians when Jesus submersed Himself in a life with them. He lived with them, among them. He was with them enough to be sometimes annoyed by them, yet He had compassion on them. They were His best friends. He took them with Him up a mountain to pray just before He was crucified. Instead of praying, they fell asleep. Then they betrayed Him when His enemies came looking for Him. Even at the end, it seems sometimes they didn't get it. It's safe to say Jesus was heavily relationally invested in frail people whose sins were abominations to God. Peter had a lying tongue and Judas had a heart that devised wicked schemes. They had haughty eyes at times. All of them, at one time or another made the abomination cut, I'm sure, but Jesus never stopped them or violated their free will. He simply broke bread while He knew full well what Judas was up to. Just because someone's sin is listed as an abomination, it doesn't give us license to disregard his or her personal choices regarding the truth.

We all have boundaries, walls, defenses. We all need space to be ourselves, make our own decisions, and express our ideas. We all have our inner circle of trusted people who can say what they want to us, and then we have those who need to build a little more trust with us to get that close.

You have to know where you stand. Maybe you're inside that circle for your loved one. I hope so. Your message will be heard with love.

If you're outside that circle, it's not hopeless. If you carry a message for them that will perhaps change who they are, you should ask permission to share with them. If they decline, give them space. Don't become defensive, or pout, or feel rejected. Just go on living in love toward them, and maybe they will see that you don't intend to violate their will. Perhaps at some point they will let you in behind their walls and hear you out. If your message is really for their benefit, and not for yours, they'll believe that more if your actions indicate patience and you display a personal security about it.

When someone feels an unstoppable need to quote Scripture to a person, or get them to listen to the Bible through a pastor, a sermon, or a book, it is almost always because they want a switch to flip on. They want that person to come to their senses, see the light, and immediately and completely change.

But grace is a gradual process, and Scripture is not a switch (the punishing or the light bulb kind).

Scripture is very powerful and it can and does wash hearts every day so the truth can take root, but it, like any other element of the gospel, has to be clothed in love and pure intention.

It's easy to tell when someone wants you to change for his or her own comfort.

It's also easy to tell when they are comfortable and at peace for their own selves, whether you see for yourself the light they are trying to share or not.

One scenario puts the truth-bringer in a powerful and persuasive position. The other just makes them look desperate. People despise desperation. They respond to power.

When I've heard of families dealing with a homosexual family member and I learn of all the first responses, so many times I hear of a father rushing his son or daughter to the pastor's house they barely know for a Bible lesson on why it's wrong to be gay. I hope it's easy to see now how this can be a big mistake from a relational perspective.

But forcing the conversation without honoring and empowering the hearer can be a mistake from a biblical perspective as well.

Follow me down a path of Scripture, if you will.

First, whatever your stance on the matter based on the ideas discussed in the Grid of Response chapter, none can argue, with reason and from a biblical perspective, that the desire to be free from homosexuality or same-sex attraction is a sin.

"But the fruit of the Spirit is love, joy, peace, forbearance, kindness, goodness, faithfulness, gentleness and self-control. Against such things there is no law. Those who belong to Christ Jesus have crucified the flesh with its passions and desires. Since we live by the Spirit, let us keep in step with the Spirit."
— *The Apostle Paul, Galatians 5:22-25*

So you have a biblical green light to preach freedom from homosexual desire. But how?

All too often we get off on the wrong foot because we make our starting point in this discussion the destruction of Sodom and Gomorrah. It is one of the main six scriptures we reference to highlight God's hatred of homosexuality and the great wrath it inspires in Him. But how closely do we look at this Scripture? I'm not talking about from a culturally relevant standpoint, but just from a thorough reading of the events plainly set forth in this passage. We place an emphasis on the destruction part, but if we look closely, I believe we can see more of an emphasis on mercy than destruction.

Just before the destruction of the cities, The Lord and two angels came down and appeared to Abraham, promising him and Sarah they would be the father of many nations. As that scene was ending and the men were getting up to leave, Abraham got up and walked along with them to see them on their way. Get the picture of that with me — the Lord and a couple of angels are visiting, and Abe just walks them out, the same way we walk our friends out to their car when they leave our house. The men are glancing off into the distance at their next destination when, almost as if it's an afterthought, the Lord said (Genesis 18:17), *"Shall I hide from Abraham what I am about to do? Abraham will surely become a great and powerful nation, and all nations on earth will be blessed through him."*

In terms we can understand from the business world, Abraham had just made partner, and the CEO was asking him to weigh in on the firm's next big move. It's like the Lord is telling the angels, "Well boys, I guess I need to give Abraham a say in this decision, because he has influence now."

That is the first revolutionary moment in this passage. God was now partnering with man and Abraham had a voice in the destiny of an entire city.

The Lord shared with him in Genesis 18:20 that, *"The outcry against Sodom and Gomorrah is so great and their sin so grievous that I will go down and see if what they have done is as bad as the outcry that has reached me. If not, I will know."*

Here is another revolutionary concept: God heard an outcry, but He didn't just strike the city with lightning and move on. He actually took the time to appear in the flesh. He conferred with Abraham about it, and sent an investigative party to go and see, and be among them. *He put his messengers at great personal risk to evaluate the conditions on the ground.*

So back to this scene — the two angels kept walking but the Lord and Abraham stood there, negotiating. And this is the third revolutionary moment in this passage. I find it completely antithetical to our modern religious culture that the first act of this newly appointed father of nations was to plead for mercy for the unrighteous.

The cities were destroyed in the end, as we know, but I wonder if when we preach this passage we miss the greater point. Do we adequately reflect on the role that is specific to us, in our time? As believers in the covenant of grace, we are charged to disciple nations. Therefore, we should most identify with Abraham in this story. And Abraham's position on the matter out of his role as father to nations and partner with God was *intercession that advocated for mercy.* So often I think we over-identify with the righteous who escaped the fire, and that's not entirely inaccurate, but there is an even better perspective to be seen here than our usual position. Normally we look at the story from the perspective of city dwellers and hold tightly to the promise of deliverance from judgment if we remain righteous in a heathen culture. There's truth in that, but we forget that Lot's family had actually *chosen* to live in that culture. They obviously didn't hate it because his wife looked back, as we recall, on the comfort she was abandoning as they fled the city. It wasn't easy for her to leave. The righteous were delivered from the destruction, as is typically the outcome throughout Scripture. That's a promise that's threaded throughout the Bible, so we can take comfort in that, but we should also see that many times, the righteous had chosen to be among them.

I get a sense of the posture we could take toward culture from this passage, don't you? We could make intercession for our culture before God, we could prefer mercy, and we could go and walk vulnerably among the people in an unbelieving and sometimes violent atmosphere.

All through the Bible, before a city or a nation was judged, God always sent a messenger to be among the people and see if things were as they seemed. God has always sought redemption first. He did this with Jeremiah, on Jerusalem's behalf. In Jeremiah 5:1, God said, *"Go up and down the streets of Jerusalem, look around and consider, search through her squares. If you can find but one person who deals honestly and seeks the truth, I will forgive this city."*

He did this with Jonah, on Nineveh's behalf. I find this story interesting because it adds nuance to our modern conceptions on what it means to preach repentance. I think it's ironic that God chose a man who hated Nineveh to bring salvation to them, and to the messenger as well. When God called Jonah, He said to go and cry out against the city because their wickedness had come up before Him. Jonah immediately boarded a ship to run from the assignment. But God wasn't moved in His intentions, so He brought a storm and, after some discussion, Jonah's fellow travelers threw him off the ship. Then a great fish swallowed Jonah, and he had a change of heart while he was camping out in its belly. When Jonah was spit up on the land, God again said, *"Go to the great city of Nineveh and proclaim to it the message I give you." (Jonah 3:1)* God didn't even tell him the exact message until he got there. Turns out, like Sodom, the city was going to be destroyed in forty days (no mention of homosexuality as the cause of destruction). The cool part is the plan worked, and the people repented and declared a fast! True to His nature, God was merciful and changed His plan. *"Then God saw their works, that they turned from their evil way; and God relented from the disaster that He had said He would bring upon them, and He did not do it."* (Jonah 3:10) But Jonah was angry because it seemed unjust to him. In Scripture's exact words, *"But it displeased Jonah exceedingly, and he became angry. So he prayed to the LORD, and said, 'Ah, LORD, was not this what I said when I was still in my country? Therefore I fled previously to Tarshish; for I know that You are a gracious and merciful God, slow to anger and abundant in lovingkindness, One who relents from doing harm. Therefore now, O LORD, please take my life from me, for it is better for me to die than to live!"* Wow. Jonah knew the Lord was merciful and full of grace, and he didn't want to see Nineveh treated with that kind of lovingkindness. It's almost like he *wanted* the city to be destroyed. He wanted it so badly that he wanted to die when the plans for destruction changed. Hmmm. Is that how we feel about the immorality in our own culture? God's heart shines through when He says in the last verse of Jonah, *"And should I not pity Nineveh, that great city, in which are more than one hundred and twenty thousand persons who cannot discern between their right hand and their left?"* Are we getting the picture that God has compassion for those who live in immorality because they are without discernment?

This message is so rich for the Church right now. The list of people in the Bible sent to be among unredeemed and wicked cultures is long, and the thread of God's mercy and lovingkindness is woven tightly around every one of these stories in Scripture. Commonly, we are able to identify with the judgment and the cry for repentance, but we should look again at all of these scenarios and find the mercy and the intentional interaction. In all of these scenarios, the separation theories we use to justify lack of relationship lose their ability to hold water. God's people took great risk and did the hard work of engaging their cultures. I believe if the Church can see this, it will inform our response to the issue of homosexuality in our day and exponentially increase the chance that people will lean into mercy exponentially. Jesus is the final culmination of this theme of God dwelling among men to bring redemption. Again, the men He called to His side were not Christians. He drafted unredeemed men who were burdened with the problems common to man, and lived full time with them. He came and dwelt among us to save us all for the purpose of bringing us into relationship with Himself and the Father.

When Jesus was addressing the city of Capernaum in Matthew 11, He said an interesting thing:

"And you, Capernaum, will you be lifted to the heavens? No, you will go down to Hades. For if the miracles that were performed in you had been performed in Sodom, it would have remained to this day. But I tell you that it will be more bearable for Sodom on the day of judgment than for you."

Capernaum is well known as Jesus' home base during the time of His ministry. It's where He called Simon Peter to His side as He walked the docks. There, He healed an entire city at the home of Peter's mother-in-law on the first night of Peter's discipleship in ministry. Countless miracles were performed. Love was demonstrated. Healings, resurrections, and the most inspired teachings of Jesus' life were all given in this tiny region, a fishing village on the shore of the Sea of Galilee.

And what was His message to them, when it was all said and done?

"Sodom would have repented if they'd been given your opportunities."

Nevermind what Capernaum did wrong for now. If we seek the depth of this verse, it's *what Sodom would have done right if given Capernaum's opportunities.*

Jesus was introducing a better way. The Old Testament is marked with messengers of repentance and cities turning or burning, but Jesus was about to change the game. Instead of continuing in the vein of sending messengers to preach repentance and make destruction threats over and over again, He was unpacking a new method that would bring a lasting change to the hearts who could hear and believe. And while there is much to be gained from the repentance prophets and preachers, the fruit was never lasting. Sodom was sent the two angels. The angels were lusted after and at risk of physical harm, so the city was destroyed. Similarly, the reluctant Jonah was sent to Nineveh in a whale's belly. They repented for a little while, but at another time in Scripture the city was destroyed anyway because they went right back to their old ways. And how many countless prophets were assigned to the perpetually unrepentant Israel? Just before the grand opening of the new covenant, John the Baptist preached repentance and it opened eyes, but in the end they had his head.

I'm not necessarily saying there's no place for preaching repentance, ever, but the demonstration of the power of God was Jesus' chosen primary method of delivering the gospel. He was saying that compassion produced a power that would have captured the heart of Sodom.

Paul said it this way to the Corinthians: *"When I came to you, I did not come with eloquence or human wisdom as I proclaimed to you the testimony about God. For I resolved to know nothing while I was with you except Jesus Christ and Him crucified. I came to you in weakness with great fear and trembling. My message and my preaching were not with wise and persuasive words, but with a demonstration of the Spirit's power, so that your faith might not rest on human wisdom, but on God's power."* — Paul, 1 Corinthians 2:1-5

Paul then goes on to say to those who invited and welcomed him into their lives: *"We do, however, speak a message of wisdom among the mature..."* It seems Paul is indicating that the place for repentance speeches is among those who are mature in the truth but are not obeying. But again, the message of repentance is delivered in the context of relationship, trust, and permission.

So Paul follows Jesus in showing us that power wins. Power is interesting because it never stands alone. It has a partner each time it makes an appearance.

If you have studied the life of Jesus, you will know that almost without fail, each time power was demonstrated and a miracle was performed, the Bible documents that "Jesus was moved with compassion," or "Jesus had compassion on the crowds." Many times, the compassion was notable because it was clear that in His humanity, Jesus would have preferred to be alone. One specific time, it was when He was grieving over the senseless killing of his dear friend John the Baptist, whose head was cut off because the king was seduced. When many would have burned with injustice and anger, Jesus found compassion for an entire multitude.

The point is, Jesus was in some tight spots when He had to dig down deep, bring compassion from Heaven's throne room, and demonstrate the kind of power that defies nature. Now that's how you earn ears and win hearts, ladies and gentlemen!

Many times in our culture (ahem, Facebook rants), you see people — even prominent leaders — condemning sin and speaking about the downfall of Sodom and Gomorrah as an imminent parallel for America because of the homosexual issues we face. We have a religious zeal and a fervor for speaking out against something. It's really easy to do when we aren't personally affected by the issue we're soapboxing about.

But it's not productive... at all. Sometimes power means holding your tongue. Sometimes power is restrained strength. Sometimes power is meekness and humility.

I want to look more closely at the source of zeal behind a lot of social media rants because they often turn into fights resulting in the loss of relationship between Christians and unbelievers.

Going back to the passage in Matthew, just prior to the verses where Jesus is addressing Capernaum and speaking of the effectiveness of miracles, there is a passage that has incorrectly fueled many religious fires.

Matthew 11:12 says, *"And from the days of John the Baptist until now the kingdom of heaven suffers violence, and the violent take it by force. For all the prophets and the law prophesied until John."*

Many well-intentioned Christians who feel intimidated, afraid, and victimized by the rise of non-Christian worldview in American culture over the past several decades have used this reference to legitimize a violent attitude toward anything that appears to threaten the establishment of God's kingdom in culture.

But I don't think that's what this verse is commissioning.

Jesus is saying that the kingdom of heaven is a hard thing for us to enter into. He's saying this at the end of a long response to a question from the messengers that worked for John the Baptist, who want to know if it is He whom John was prophesying about. He's been answering the messengers with stories about His miracles, saying:

"The blind see and the lame walk; the lepers are cleansed and the deaf hear; the dead are raised up and the poor have the gospel preached to them. And blessed is he who is not offended because of Me." — Jesus, Matthew 11:5, 6

He goes on to say that John was not a reed shaken by the wind, or a man clothed in soft garments. Nope, John was hard core. He was a prophet, and more than a prophet. Jesus says there was not a greater man before John the Baptist.

But then He tells us: *"He who is least in the kingdom of heaven is greater than he [John the Baptist]."*

That is a powerful statement.

Whoever is least in this new covenant with Jesus is greater than John.

And *then* comes the violence verse.

He's saying it's hard to get in. It's like black Friday and mobs are piled up at the door to take advantage of the sales. It's hard to get in, and instead of squeezing through crowds and doors, the barrier we have to violently force our way past is our own sin nature. It's a tough go of killing your flesh to be made a disciple. It's about YOU. *Your heart.* Not your neighbor's.

Luke 16:16 says it better, *"The Law and the Prophets were proclaimed until John. Since that time, the good news of the kingdom of God is being preached, and everyone is forcing their way into it."*

The kingdom is such a good thing, full of so much good news that people are clamoring to get in, once they understand. The next verse in Luke speaks of the Law (Old Testament) not easily disappearing. People want the grace that redeems them and counts them righteous.

Jesus gave this good news through love and a model of honoring men when He didn't feel like it. He ensured the law was known, but He did not use it as the primary channel of forming relationship or as a prequalification for those He would give His life and love to.

Does this help us with the violence thing? Does it free us from some of our culture warrior mindset?

If you live in a modern day Sodom and want to see it change, are you forcing your way into the miraculous kingdom of God and living in God's power and love toward those around you?

If we truly love and understand the message of freedom, we'll do the hard work of telling it from a position of permission and trust in a person's life. We'll get inside. Build trust. Take our time. Positional authority as pastors or even parents means nearly nothing when it comes to changing hearts. Authentic relationship has to occupy the space created by positional proximity. If there's work to do on the trust front, start there.

To the lovers go the prize of hearts.

Also stated: *The meek shall inherit the earth.*

Shame and Anger

Few things are more debilitating in this life than the weight of shame. The Bible employs over twenty-two words in both Hebrew and Greek over the course of its sixty-six book narrative to fully expose its impact on humanity.

To scratch the surface, according to Strong's Concordance, shame can mean: a base, filthy, disgraceful obscenity or dishonesty; to give cause for rebuke, to bring reproach, or to blush through the idea of detection; disappointed, confounded, brought to confusion; the feeling or condition of shame, disgrace, confusion, dishonor, reproach; to wound, taunt, insult, to make ashamed, to make blush, to cause to be confounded, to be hurt.

With such an array of soul-torturing devices, it's easy to see why many people manufacture a self-protective form of pride to avoid the psychological defeat and sometimes literal death produced by a heart and mind imprisoned in shame's interrogation rooms. This protective coping mechanism is often expressed in the form of anger, indignation, an intellectual or moral elitism, or a combination of these which all serve the end of undermining or overriding the value of the perceived source of shame.

I want to unpack shame a little bit. It's one of the major reasons people who struggle with same-sex attraction aren't able to maintain close relationships with those who don't understand why they can't easily change. It keeps many vital relationships with family and friends at bay for one who struggles, and it's important then to gain a full understanding of the dynamics of shame.

The book of Job is a powerful illustration of the strength of shame: *"If I am guilty — woe to me! Even if I am innocent, I cannot lift my head, for I am full of shame and drowned in my affliction."* — Job 10:15

This verse brings up an interesting point. Shame can be present and have its life-altering effects on a person whether it is deserved or not, whether we are guilty of an offense or not.

God equipped all of mankind with a certain capacity for shame, so it obviously has a purpose — to protect us from the consequences of life outside the safety of the grace of God. Shame's intended purpose is to protect us in a sinful moment. It produces a corrective response in us, then fades once we've set things right. But when we hear this internal voice we call our conscience and fail to heed its direction, we can effectively turn down its volume over time. We can continue to override this corrective force and sear it into a state of complete unresponsiveness.

Jeremiah 6:15 illustrates this truth: *"'Are they ashamed of their detestable conduct? No, they have no shame at all; they do not even know how to blush. So they will fall among the fallen; they will be brought down when I punish them,' says the Lord."*

Zephaniah 3:5 says, *"The Lord within her is righteous; He does no wrong. Morning by morning He dispenses His justice, and every new day He does not fail, yet the unrighteous know no shame."*

To be clear, these verses are not describing a total absence of shame. Instead, they describe a lack of response to it. They speak to the fact that in God's eyes, shame should be present, but they appear to have no indication that it is because they do not repent or take heed of the mercy available every morning.

The problem with living in this state of unresponsiveness to shame is that the weight of shame is not proportional to the decibel level of the voice of conscience. Rather, it is responsive to the culture and context we live in, and for the Christian, to the immutable laws of God and righteousness. A life lived in stark contrast to the mores of the times or biblical principles of holiness will still be marked with some measure of shame because we cannot help but define and measure ourselves by each other and by external standards. For those who reject biblical standards, this explains the compulsive need to continually alter our culture's acceptance of homosexuality.

As humans we are drawn to tribes. This is the reason for the powerful attractiveness of groups which form around causes. The more in contrast the group's cause is to the norms of society, the more likely that group is to be working out a plan to gain acceptance in culture. They are often angry, violent, obstinate, or elitist in an effort to drown out the shame. I wonder what would happen if we could always remember this, and trained ourselves to respond to a shame-based plea for legitimacy with honor and compassion. Would it help shape a new dialogue in culture? Wisdom would note that this is just as true a statement for a radical fundamentalist religious group as it would be for a radical left wing liberal gay rights group. Both can easily function out of a desire to end their shame. In fact, much of the culture wars we see over LGBT causes are rooted in each group seeking to undermine the validity of the other's existence.

Contrary to our emotional reflexes and what conventional wisdom would have us believe, the opposite of shame is not pride. It is humility. Humility has the effect of healing shame by separating a person from their actions. Humility is an expression of objectivity — it affirms our value as a person while allowing us space for adjusting our actions to line up with the call of conscience. Pride perpetuates shame because it traps us into a form of subjectivity — a belief that our actions are a part of us, innately valuable and sometimes unchangeable, whether sinful or not. Rather than lose face when we ourselves, or others, disagree with the moral appropriateness of our actions, pride imprisons us to defend our actions as part of who we are. By taking this stance, pride introduces an element of personal rejection and creates conflict for those who view our actions as wrong but still value us as a person and want to love us. Because all of humanity is instinctively aware that humility is an option, when we choose pride, we bring the low esteem of shame upon our character instead of only our actions. Anything short of humility perpetuates a cycle of constant self-defensive response to the sources of shame within culture and conscience, and brings a permanent residence to the devices of shame that are only designed to be temporary in visitation. This cycle eventually puts us at war within because we are, on some level, giving credence to the voice of conscience that is set against us because we must continually seek to override it as the source of our shame. This places a weight upon the soul that we are not intended to bear, and it can even have drastic effects on our physical health.

Daniel 12:2 paints an interesting picture that actually equates shame to hell: *"Multitudes who sleep in the dust of the earth will awake: some to everlasting life, others to shame and everlasting contempt."* This passage brings into the foreground the great bearing shame can have upon our souls by contrasting it with everlasting life. It's my belief that we create a veritable hell on earth for ourselves when we live in a secured state of prideful allegiance to our actions. We become isolated and tormented by the process of vying for worth against the voice of conscience and our very personalities can begin to change to become what some know as shame-based.

It's at this point that many people are tempted, as I described in my story, to lay down on the mat and quit. Pride's temptation to turn struggle into statement, to come out and just be proud of my sexuality, worked almost artfully on my soul. The touch of shame upon my heart was almost electric at times. It's heaviness was so much at work in me, particularly after a moral failure, that I longed for relief from conviction, and was tempted to achieve it by aligning myself with a darker wisdom that told me it was okay to quit fighting, that I couldn't change. But, I knew an agreement like that would set me at enmity with God. I didn't know exactly why or how at the time, but I knew it would. The first chapter of Romans states several times that the mind of the unbelieving is eventually "given over" to the darkness it chooses to embrace. This always seemed to be the worst thing that could happen to me — that God would allow me to move fully into a deception I couldn't gain objectivity over. It struck a holy fear in me.

Philippians 3:18 describes it in this way, *"Many live as enemies of the cross of Christ. Their destiny is destruction, their god is their stomach, and their **glory is in their shame**. Their mind is set on earthly things."*

Hopefully this description of the process and effects of shame can bring to focus what the sons and daughters of God who fight homosexuality are going through.

But they are not the only ones enduring shame.

The families of those who fight are also subject to the persuasions and judgments of culture. All throughout my journey, my family remained acutely aware of the growing polarity between cultural and religious positions on homosexuality. Even though they spent years in silence over my struggle, incidental comments and opinions expressed by others on the subject of homosexuality almost always heaped more condemnation and shame upon them. While they do not subscribe to the acceptability of homosexuality, they also did not experience a compassionate spirit from others for those who are faced with the reality of having a loved one struggle with it. Staying silent was a protective strategy for all of us, but it was not without the consequences of isolation, with shame as our frequent visitor.

My parents went through years of torment, questioning their methods and wondering what in the world they could have done to save me or prevent this tragedy. Accusation was at the doorstep of their hearts with every glance cast askew at them and every rumor that surfaced regarding me.

As a family, our individual senses of shame played off each other. Any time my parents would ask me what they did wrong, I would recoil into a place of greater shame because it was embarrassing for me to feel that I gave them any cause for questioning themselves. It was a relentless and burdensome process, and I assume it would be for any set of people who try to figure out how one person's sin begets another's. In the end, we are all responsible for our own actions and affixing blame to another for our state of being is never productive. Fortunately, we saw that happening, and we were more committed to maintaining common ground and a sense of peace, so we didn't overanalyze ourselves or our relationships when times were at their toughest. Somehow, instinctively, and through the Spirit of God, we just recognized that each of us were in a process of reconciling our present reality to our faith, and we trusted that everyone was doing their best.

Unfortunately, this grace does not visit every family, and many parents and family members become very reactive when they feel the shame heaped upon them by their loved one's affliction. Even if a family member is set on fighting this in their life and achieving victory through celibacy or reorientation, parents can be subject to the helplessness of feeling the reproach of another person's sin. There is injustice in the shame because the family cannot do one thing to change their collective situation, except simply wait, extend unconditional love and pray.

Because they are not able to change their son or daughter, both passive and aggressive anger often become a mainstay in communication for families dealing with this situation. This loops us back into the discussion on fear and religion's methods of creating forceful situations to try to bring superficial change. Shame, fear, religion, anger — these are forces that all work together for the destruction of families. These are so deadly and such successful devices of the enemy because the son or daughter, in their own war against shame, will distance themselves or even cut ties with the parent whose response is based in anger because it reinforces the hellacious experience of their embattled existence.

There is HOPE. Both for the families and their loved ones.

Psalm 34:5 says, *"Those who look to Him are radiant; their faces are never covered with shame."*

When we let God take up our family's cause and defend our honor for us, shame is removed. And, different from shame-based pride, there is a righteous pride that refuses to accept the effects of shame. This is revealed in Isaiah 50:7, which says, *"Because the Sovereign Lord helps me, I will not be disgraced. Therefore have I set my face like flint, and I know I will not be put to shame."*

Isaiah 54:4 says, *"Do not be afraid; you will not be put to shame. Do not fear disgrace; you will not be humiliated. You will forget the shame of your youth and remember no more the reproach of your widowhood."*

Sometimes it's true that for whatever reason, we are not equipped to deal with our circumstances. Sometimes it's true that abusive family environments are, in part, to blame for sexual identity issues. In these situations, we deal with them however we can at the time because the instinct for survival is very real. In this, we take up our own causes instead of looking to our Father. Later in life, we come to a place of greater understanding: that He hates the injustice, robbery, and wrongdoing that hurt and shamed us. God will vindicate us with honor when the circumstances of life have victimized us for shame.

Isaiah 61:7, 8 promises this, *"Instead of your shame you will receive a double portion, and instead of disgrace you will rejoice in your inheritance. And so you will inherit a double portion in your land, and everlasting joy will be yours. For I, the Lord, love justice; I hate robbery and wrongdoing. In my faithfulness I will reward my people and make an everlasting covenant with them."*

For all the work shame does to destroy our inner peace, undermine our consciences, and leave us in victimized torment, the grace of God empowers us to stand up in unbelievable strength to overcome and reverse the damage. The beauty of our relationship with God lies in the fact that our dignity is not rooted in our successful actions, but in the successful alignment of our hearts with the covenant of peace God offers us through the redemptive work Jesus did on the cross. Christ has liberated us from the power that binds us to pride and has reconciled us to God forever, without regard to our former shame. The justification through faith described in the Bible is the source of our power as humans to choose humility in dealing with our own shortcomings and severing our character from our actions when our actions betray us. Pride is replaced by a confidence in the Lord's unconditional embrace of our value as people.

Both Parents and those struggling with homosexuality can draw great strength from Romans 5:1-5, which summarizes this mystery: *"Therefore, since we have been justified through faith, we have peace with God through our Lord Jesus Christ, through whom we have gained access by faith into this grace in which we now stand. And we boast in the hope of the glory of God. Not only so, but we also glory in our sufferings, because we know that suffering produces perseverance; perseverance, character; and character, hope. And hope does not put us to shame, because God's love has been poured out into our hearts through the Holy Spirit, who has been given to us."*

THE QUESTIONS

Is This My Fault?

In a word: No.

No, this is not your fault.

Throughout my journey, there were those inevitable and well-intentioned voices who sought to assign the source of my homosexuality to the faults of my parents.

I have good parents. They were not just average parents who loved me and made sure I had a roof over my head and then left me on autopilot. They were involved, loving, inquisitive parents. They took me to church and made sure I felt comfortable in my youth group before they would commit to church membership based on their own desires. They made sure I did well in school. My eighth grade history class was hard for me, and when a test was coming up, Dad always read my chapters with me and, the morning of the test woke me up early to make me breakfast and quiz me down. They attended my soccer games and piano recitals and talent shows. They were present in my brother's and my life and knew how to show us a good time. We went on family vacations every summer. These were not extravagant, but they were meaningful times. My dad turned down countless positions and salary increases all over the country to provide our family with stability

— which really meant, to keep us in the churches where we were thriving, in good schools where we were excelling in academics and sports, and in relationships with good friends, where we were learning how to maneuver through social experiences.

So when I was seeking to understand how I arrived at same-sex attraction, and when people would dig for answers in my family relationships, I'd always get uncomfortable. This seems to be a knee-jerk reaction the Church has adopted from secular philosophical ideas that aren't always biblical. Yes, there is that one verse about the sins of the father being visited upon the following generations, but we tend to overthink things sometimes. I don't believe that understanding the origin of homosexuality is a necessary component to freedom. Sometimes, in fact, I think an over-emphasis on the origin can serve to keep a person bound to their identity as homosexual.

There was a time when it felt good to make sense of my struggle as the fruit of my parents' faults. After all, they aren't perfect people, so flaws were there to be found. In the end, however, when I started actually getting free from same-sex attraction, it wasn't because I forgave a gap in the character of either of my parents. I did forgive some things, but those were not singularly freeing moments. Forgiveness of parents' shortcomings is a process every adult goes through as part of emerging from the innocence of childhood into the responsibility of adulthood. If they make a conscious decision to issue forgiveness, they gain identity and power. If they refuse to, they remain a victim. That's how that works. But I don't believe that process is always core to freedom from homosexuality. In my experience, forgiveness of my parents' mistakes was not an ultimate key to my transformation. In fact, I may have spent too much time looking in that direction and delayed my own freedom. Forgiving can help, but it's all too easy to get stuck on the digging part.

"But what if I've been a horrible parent," you ask?

If you are aware of things you did to damage your kid, and you haven't already, then by all means, make amends. Apologize. State clearly what you did wrong, and how you would do it differently if you had it to do over again. If your child is still young, start doing it differently. But don't belabor the point. For relationship to get traction, you have to forgive yourself, learn to view yourself as a worthy parent, and then carry that out by assigning worth to your son or daughter and your relationship with them. It might be slow at first, but it can heal over time.

I would just like to point out that since my parents were truly focused on creating a healthy childhood for me, and I still ended up struggling with homosexuality, it serves to negate the argument that parents who have failed grossly actually "made their kid turn out gay." Environment plays a role sometimes, but not always, and we can't be too careful when it comes to assigning blame. Anyone, at anytime, can find this battle has haunted their doorstep.

Parents, your kids need you. No matter what they are saying with their words right now, in their heart they know they need you. And they need you to be the strong you.

You don't have time to maintain your regrets.

Any you know what? God is jealous for your affections. Don't give them to the demons of self-loathing.

"How He Loves" by John Mark McMillan sums up what I'm trying to say. It was written the day after his friend was unexpectedly killed. The pain of a loved one's death is similar to what we experience when the familiar face of a loved one seems to change, so I leave this question of whether this is your fault or not with Mr. McMillan's very apt words.

He is jealous for me.

Love's like a hurricane, I am a tree

Bending beneath the weight of His wind and mercy.

When all of a sudden, I am unaware of these afflictions eclipsed by glory

and I realize just how beautiful You are and how great your affections are for me.

So we are His portion and He is our prize,

Drawn to redemption by the grace in His eyes.

If grace is an ocean we're all sinking .

So heaven meets earth like a sloppy wet kiss and my heart turns violently inside of my chest .

I don't have time to maintain these regrets when I think about the way

He loves us.

Well, I thought about You the day Stephen died and You met me between my breaking

I know that I still love You, God, despite the agony

...they want to tell me You're cruel

But if Stephen could sing, he'd say it's not true, cause...

Cause He loves us,

Woah, how He loves us.

Is My Kid Going to Hell?

One of the most common fears families and individuals who struggle with homosexuality face is regarding the eternal status of their souls. For a long time, if I could have believed I would not go to hell for being a lesbian, I might have embraced it. But fear is not an enduring motivator. As we looked at shame, we saw that shame itself is a form of hell. This absolutely does not deny a literal, physical hell, but it does allude to the fact that if people are willing to become conditioned to shame which the bible positions interchangeably with hell, then it stands to reason they will not be motivated long term by an intangible awareness of punishment that awaits them in the afterlife.

Regardless, it is a worthy discussion because it can strike fear and bring instability into the situation that may not be necessary. There are no blanket answers to this question when asked in the face of any sin pattern that is ongoing, but it gets easier if we look at the heart of a person, as Jesus does.

People often say things like, "If she were really a Christian, this would not be a pattern in her life." Or, "If he really loved God, he would not desire things that God doesn't condone." It's easy to say that when you're talking about something as controversial as homosexuality, but what about gluttony? Do you desire to eat thousand calorie meals at every sitting, but restrain yourself for health reasons? Or maybe it's shame that holds you back — no one wants to be seen going back for second helpings and multiple desserts. Or what about pornography, to step it up a notch? What if it's not the motivation of love for Christ that stops you, but the Internet history that doesn't lie? Obviously this could go on to call out all forms of sin, but I think the point is simply made that a desire for sinful things doesn't negate our salvation or salvation would be unattainable for all people.

Romans 9:30-33 says, *"What then shall we say? That the Gentiles, who did not pursue righteousness, have obtained it, a righteousness that is by faith; but the people of Israel, who pursued the law as the way of righteousness, have not attained their goal. Why not? Because they pursued it not by faith but as if it were by works. They stumbled over the stumbling stone. As it is written: 'See, I lay in Zion a stone that causes people to stumble and a rock that makes them fall, and the one who believes in Him will never be put to shame.'"*

The scriptures that inform our basic concept of salvation rise up against the pervasive thought that those who cannot overcome their homosexuality are bound for hell. Those who agree that Scripture leaves no room for homosexual behavior, and believe upon Christ for the grace to be counted righteous before God as they strive to line their lives up with His lordship are counted as righteous. Like any other sinner, they will be found wanting at times when measured against the law, but like any other sinner, they will also be afforded grace if their faith is not placed in their own actions but in the redemptive power of Christ's resurrection.

The law doesn't make you righteous, or even save you. It only sets the boundaries which define the concept of righteousness.

Romans 10:4-11 states, *"Christ is the culmination of the law so that there may be righteousness for everyone who believes. Moses writes this about the righteousness that is by the law: 'The person who does these things will live by them.' But the righteousness that is by faith says: "Do not say in your heart, 'Who will ascend into heaven?'" (that is, to bring Christ down) or "'Who will descend into the deep?'" (that is, to bring Christ up from the dead). But what does it say? "The word is near you; it is in your mouth and in your heart," that is, the message concerning faith that we proclaim: If you declare with your mouth, "Jesus is Lord," and believe in your heart that God raised him from the dead, you will be saved. For it is with your heart that you believe and are justified, and it is with your mouth that you profess your faith and are saved. As scripture says, "Anyone who believes in Him will never be put to shame."*

The heart is that which believes and justifies us. And the heart is always in process for everyone who claims to be a child of God. It is by the words of our mouth that we profess this belief, even when it's difficult or unpopular, and we are saved. To be clear, this verse is not speaking of a one-time prayer we pray that creates our ticket to heaven, rather, it is with every word we speak that we are continually professing either faith or unbelief. It is from the overflow of a heart (either believing or unbelieving) that the mouth speaks, and the mouth will create either a world of unbelief and darkness that separates us from Christ, or a world of belief and light that justifies us in accordance with His covenant.

This is where I find my position that if a person's heart is turned toward God, and they are actively working out the aspects of their faith in consistent dialogue with God, they are saved. If they are tuned out and uncaring toward the voice of God that speaks life to them, well, only God can see the true condition of their heart and look beyond manifestations of rebellion, callousness, or anger that come from shame. Scripture is clear that it's not for us to question the condition of another's heart. But hope can be offered in the situation where a person truly desires the full redemption of Christ, even if life is cut short. It seems clear to me they are not going to be separated from God in eternity because they were not separated from Him on earth.

When Paul was imprisoned for his faith, he wrote to his disciple, Timothy, saying, *"That is why I am suffering as I am. Yet this is no cause for shame, because I know whom I have believed, and am convinced that He is able to guard what I have entrusted to Him until that day." (2 Timothy 1:12)*

While our loved ones and families may suffer a different kind of imprisonment — perhaps the effects of shame, or the frustration of an unchanged desire — the Bible makes it clear that our suffering is no cause for shame, and offers hope that when we place our belief in God, He will guard us until that day that judgment comes for the lives we've lived unto Him.

We must remember that punishment and suffering are not the heart of God toward His children. Through the course of the entire Bible, we see His patience stave off His anger more times than not, because God is always seeking relationship with us. He originally created us for fellowship in the first place! He always wants us, our intimacy, and our friendship.

Sometimes, our circumstances may not change until long after our hearts have. My heart was to overcome my orientation long before I experienced that change as a reality in my life. It took even longer for the manifestation of my new desires to take place because it took me some time to find my husband. We have to learn to see others as being in a process. Even when their circumstances may look no different from the exterior, their hearts may already be greatly transformed. There is no way to tell from the outside looking in. And even still, if there is no inward change, we can maintain hope because we don't lose our last valid chance for relationship and agreement with God until we draw our last breath.

Consider the scenario of the thieves who were crucified with Jesus (Luke 23:32-43). One of the criminals who hung there hurled insults at Him: "Aren't you the Messiah? Save yourself and us!"

But the other criminal rebuked him. "Don't you fear God," he said, "since you are under the same sentence? We are punished justly, for we are getting what our deeds deserve. But this man has done nothing wrong."

Then he said, "Jesus, remember me when you come into your kingdom."

Jesus answered him, "Truly I tell you, today you will be with me in paradise."

How Do I Relate to Their Partner?

This is going to be a hard pill to swallow for some. I understand why, and I empathize with the quandary a family member's same-sex relationship puts many Christians in. The difficulty arises from several angles:

"If I welcome this new person into my home, life, or family, will it send the message I am condoning this relationship or homosexuality in general? Am I not supposed to put them away from fellowship for their own good, so they can mourn and repent?"

— And —

"How can I possibly embrace this person when this type of relationship is so foreign and unreal to me? I feel like this person stole my child away from truth."

— And —

"Can I just love my child without being around the whole scenario in full?"

These are valid questions and hard to grapple with. Basically, we want to keep the relationship with our loved one intact but doing so can land us in some awkward situations. We have to figure out how to relate to this new person, who feels like the enemy, while worrying that we're going to send the message that we now accept this lifestyle choice. It's hard, and there's often pressure from our loved one to accept this change quickly, which only adds to the stress.

I think the situation is very different if it's your child, and they are a minor. But most of the time, this situation arises with an adult son or daughter, and it can get sticky. Rather than be prescriptive for your situation since I'm not a parent, let me tell you another part of my story.

When I was a teenager, I met a lady who was mentoring my girlfriend at the time. My girlfriend had been in the midst of meeting regularly with her to try to sort out her homosexuality when I came into the picture. I really interrupted the process, and I'm sure my arrival on the scene felt like a huge setback to a really good thing that was happening. Despite the fact that she was like a mother to my girlfriend, she was careful never to let on that I was a burden or unwelcome in their lives. I really liked something about this woman, and I was intrigued at the noticeable lack of rejection toward me.

At some point, she agreed to meet with me and pray with me and my girlfriend, together, at church. I'd asked to meet that way because I wanted to know what it was like to be prayed for and to see if she would pray with both of us present. Honestly, I was probably testing the boundaries of her acceptance. During that prayer time, I mostly stared at my shoes. I didn't say much, but I listened, and I was open to God speaking to me or even changing me. I kind of hoped He would, but nothing felt different when we were done. As we were leaving, I asked her if she would pray that I could be sorry for the way I felt. I just didn't feel bad about the relationship (yet), and I knew repentance was really unattainable until I had a sense of conviction. That's all I could think to ask.

I didn't know it at the time, but it really cut her deep to hear me say that. Years later — ten years, to be exact — she asked if we could go to lunch to discuss that day because the pain still lingered. She needed to uncap the emotions she felt that day as I drove off into the sunset without remorse for the loss she was experiencing. No doubt! I can only imagine.

But when I was still vulnerable, she didn't let the pain stop her from relating to me. I'm not sure why she stuck with me, but even long after my relationship with this girlfriend was over, she stayed in my life. In fact, for a long time she was my only connection to Christianity or church while I questioned much of what I was taught growing up. In lengthy phone (sometimes multiple calls a week), she listened to my stories of pain and kept me company at a very vulnerable time in my life. She taught me about grace and love. She taught me how to study the Bible with a Strong's Concordance. She taught me about speaking in tongues and worshiping in the Spirit and so many other things that empowered my freedom. She sent me audio cassettes with teaching on them. Out of sheer boredom, I would transcribe entire messages, stopping and playing and rewinding the cassette to catch every word. I'd then underline the words that seemed interesting, and write out definitions from my Bible Dictionary. This occupied so many lonely Friday and Saturday nights when I lived alone in Dallas. I was depressed and directionless and her care packages not only gave me something to do, they gave me life. This jewel of a woman has been the connecting point that bridged me to the life I know today in many ways.

I tell you this story because I don't know where I'd be today without that kind of sacrificial love. I was not a desired character in her story, but she let me in anyway. God put me in her path and she obediently loved me out of honor for God.

We make our lives too hard if we try to do more than just love the people who come into our world — wanted or not.

And about the question of whether fellowship equates to condoning — it was never unclear that this wonderful woman did not condone or approve of homosexuality. It was always clear that she was loving me anyway, believing in a brighter future for me. And that was so much more powerful than if she'd spent time reiterating an already known point of view, or protected herself from the difficult circumstance of knowing me. She went way outside her comfort zone for me, and I was always keenly aware of that sacrifice. It inspired honor and trust and loyalty that remains to this day. Without that kind of risky, radical love, these pages would have never been written.

It's OK if you need to ask your family member or friend for some time to adjust to the new ideas on your plate. Setting boundaries and asking them to meet you part way is a great first step. It's OK to set forth some initial clarity: "This makes me uncomfortable, and I haven't changed my belief that same-sex relationships are wrong, but I love you and I want you in my life." Continually reiterating that position, though, and subsequently refusing to be in any kind of relational context is not going to send the message of unconditional love. "Unconditional" is meaningless as an adjective for love until there are situations that would be more comfortable *with* conditions, and you bravely refuse to use them. Love is real when both parties take a risk and have faith that God's grace — the stuff that brings salvation and change — is being empowered through that step of faith toward each other.

Ephesians 2:4-10 speaks of how Christ did this for us. He loved us, made us alive, and seated us with Him even while we were dead in our sins.

4 But because of his great love for us, God, who is rich in mercy, 5 made us alive with Christ even when we were dead in transgressions—it is by grace you have been saved. 6 And God raised us up with Christ and seated us with him in the heavenly realms in Christ Jesus, 7 in order that in the coming ages he might show the incomparable riches of his grace, expressed in his kindness to us in Christ Jesus. 8 For it is by grace you have been saved, through faith—and this is not from yourselves, it is the gift of God— 9 not by works, so that no one can boast. ¹⁰ For we are God's handiwork, created in Christ Jesus to do good works, which God prepared in advance for us to do.

May we likewise choose love, giving life to the dead by audacious hope, and seat them among us to show them the incomparable riches of grace.

GETTING SUPPORT

Where to Go From Here

The letter my dad wrote to his friends referenced the fact that when families face this issue, it can be the perfect storm — an opportunity for the whole family to fall apart.

There is another, more famous storm we're familiar with. It happened on the Sea of Galilee, a few thousand years ago.

Jesus was in the boat.

You know which one I'm talking about.

A storm came, and Jesus slept. But the disciples, well... they freaked out. And we like to make fun of them for that. I mean, it seems pretty obvious. They had just come from watching Jesus heal the Roman centurion's servant who understood authority and power so well that he didn't even ask Jesus to come on site to do His work. Jesus credited him with more faith than He'd seen up to that point and healed his servant from afar.

The disciples on this stormy sea were familiar with His compassion, His power, and His miracles. Jesus saw to it that their lives were full of opportunities. In fact, right after this storm, they were going to watch Him heal a daughter who wasn't dead, but sleeping, and shock a whole family by moving them in an instant right out of mourning into joy!

But at the time when *their* storm came, His power had mainly solved other people's problems. It hadn't directly affected their own faith because of their own need, in this exact type of situation.

Their lives were in danger, it was dark, and this was new. It happens every day, in many kinds of storms.

It is often those of us closest to the Solution who freak out the most and forget His track record, until Jesus jumps in our boat and calms our storms.

Then it's real.

You might say that much of their journey as disciples was one big perfect storm designed for wiping out the fear and religion that would prevent them from knowing His love and power, and then spreading the good news of that to those who needed it.

And you might find that's true of your journey through this struggle with a family member. Right next to Jesus, understanding His love and power, is the very safest place our perfect storms can find us.

Bill Johnson, pastor at Bethel Church in Redding, California, said something one time that changed my perspective on this struggle, and any challenge I will ever face. He said (paraphrased), "When you encounter a struggle or a grief, embrace that as a time when you are being privileged to allow Jesus to pull you up to His chest and comfort you in a way you've never experienced before. Embrace the opportunity to know Jesus in a new way. And in this way, you can find the power to be thankful in any circumstance." Your perspective of who Jesus is expands with every difficulty life throws your way. As He speaks to each new circumstance, and as you see the Father's role in each new scenario, you come to know God as a multi-faceted, very complex Creator. You find yourself growing by greater degrees into His image, and you start to understand that this might be the whole point.

You are going to need support. You cannot keep this a secret between you and your loved one. It is dangerous to try to do so because you are human, and some days, you're going to need a safe place to vent, scream, and cry. It's not fair to ask that person to be the one who sees you through this. They aren't going to be able to bear up under the weight of your grief, or avoid spinning off your shame into their own pain. I didn't like it, but when I was going through the thick of my trials, I knew there were a very select few that my parents spoke with, and I knew they needed it. I trusted them to protect me by being wise about whom they talked to. They could have reached out more, but they were cautious.

If you don't have that in your life, my family is starting a support community on this book's website for people who need someone to talk to. We're not licensed counselors or anything like that, but we're real people who have been through real trials, and we have other parents with similar stories signed on to help. People who join will be asked to sign a non-disclosure agreement, protecting the identity of other group members. We're just trying to be a safe place to ask questions, discuss, and grow together. We're small, but we're here, so please come join us. You'll be able to pray for others and offer insight from your own stories and strength. We'll just help each other.

To get the connection started, my parents have contributed their very powerful stories in the pages that follow. They are amazing people who weathered this storm, not perfectly, but with grace and love. We had our difficulties, but I hope you find courage and hope for your own family as you see the work God has done to keep our family strong and in unity. In the coming pages, you'll hear from my mom and learn about her emotional experiences, and the grief she fought. You'll be inspired by God's speaking to her and the promises she clung to. You'll hear from my dad and glean from the wisdom and insight he leaned on to keep himself in a place of balance. His father's heart toward me and my brother reflect the true nature of our Heavenly Father's heart. I leave you with his story because the Father's heart is what we most need connection to, and I want his words to linger with you. Please, drink deeply from their stories and then come find us on the website and add your piece to the conversation. The website is firststepsout.com. You can find more information in the back of the book.

Before I go, I want to say... I'm honored to walk with you in this journey. I said it before, but I'll say it again — I don't take it lightly to speak into your situation or into this conversation in Church and culture. I have prayed through every turn of phrase in this book, and I have done my best to tune my pen to the heart of the Father. I hope to have created a space for reflection on how we can respond constructively to a loved one's struggle. My prayer is that honor will become a natural response through an increase in understanding. I hope to have released a clear call for hope and dignity to those who needed to be told "it's OK to fight," and also need the freedom to be in process. I hope I have given you reason to hope. I pray we, together, learn to think, and to consider what love looks like. I pray you are free to acknowledge grief. I pray the chains of fear, religion, shame, and anger are broken for you. I pray I've inspired you to faith and new warmth for your family, and to faith in a new kind of Church. I long to see the dialogue surrounding homosexuality and same-sex attraction resolve to a peaceful, compassionate dialogue that is articulate in the complexity of the issue and still steadfast in the simplicity of the gospel.

Above all else, I pray you know the most important gift you can give your loved one is unconditional love. The most important thing you also need to hear is that you, also, are loved — unconditionally, and without judgment for the things you are going through. This is not your fault, and you are not alone.

Together, we have hope.

Mom's Story

The music stopped the day she walked out the door. There was always the sound of music coming from her guitar or the boom box as she dressed each day. I wept with sadness. I could not stop the pain any more than I could keep her from going; nor did I want to keep her home because it was so hard to watch her go through this thing that I did not even want to face myself. Perhaps moving away from this town would clear things up and give her time to heal. I was so thankful for her former youth director's wife for reaching out to her and inviting her to stay with them for awhile. Surely, that would fix things. That was my prayer anyway.

Let me back up a bit. For several months I had been having a very strong suspicion that something was just not the "way it should be." Actually, I had these feelings for several years in moments that hinted she was hiding something, or acting in ways that seemed too cozy with her girlfriends. But, no, she was my strong, "stand up for your faith" daughter. And, after all, I had done all the right things to teach her right from wrong, hadn't I?

I was so disappointed for her that the guys she had a crush on just always seemed to pass her by for the other girls. I always had prayed for her "future husband" and trusted God that just the right man would be there for her in His timing for her life.

But, the suspicion grew stronger and I felt the need to know for sure. I wanted to help if indeed there was a problem.

At least that is how I rationalized the new low point in my life.

I knew she spent hours journaling her thoughts, so what better way to find out? So I snooped. The shame and guilt I felt was sickening. I am not sure if it was because it confirmed my worst fear, or if it was because I had violated her privacy. Now I did not know what to do with the information.

I cried in silence for days.

I could not tell my husband for fear he would not forgive me for snooping on my grown daughter and I knew he was in denial. I had mentioned my suspicions to him in the past and he did not even want to think that was a possibility.

What was I to do but PRAY and PRAY and CRY in silence?

She would be so angry with me if I told her I had snooped. Our relationship was already tense. I attributed it to us being two strong-willed women living under the same roof, or just the typical mother vs. daughter teenage years. I finally couldn't stand it anymore and confided in my sister-in-law. She prayed with me and kept my confidence.

Soon, I confided in my husband. I really hated to break his heart, but he had to know. Maybe he already suspected. We talked at length about what to do. Were there counselors we could go to? We did not want to go to our pastor because he knew those involved. We didn't want to bring pain to their families or bring shame to our Christian daughter in her own church, so we reached out to our former pastor and a precious older prayer warrior friend of the family who taught our daughter in kindergarten and had a special love for her.

We finally had the confrontation.

"You must end this relationship and stop living this way. We can't tolerate this under our roof. We love you and will help you, but you know it's wrong and you need to stop."

How clueless we were as to how hard this was for her, too.

She must have been in such agony for so long and we had our heads in the sand. We loved her and supported her and lavished attention on her all through her growing up years. We never missed a soccer game, an award ceremony or any function she was in. We took her to church — even changed churches — to ensure she had a youth group to belong to. We spent time talking to her and supporting her with money and prayer as she went on mission trips.

Still, we blamed ourselves for leaving a deficit as parents in her life.

My husband and I prayed for our daughter together aloud and individually. That prayer seemed to annoy her and she even laughed with her friend one day as they passed by us on their way out the door together. She did not want to receive it. She was not ready to change, nor did she seem to desire change while living with us.

So, after her second college year she moved out.

We hugged and told one another how much we cared and we assured her we would be there for her and pray for her. And PRAY we did.

For years we prayed and cried and kept silent. Not even our church friends were approachable from our perspective. We felt things like that had no tolerance in our church. Surely the extended family did not suspect, did they? We covered for her and suffered in silence. You just didn't talk about things like that 15 years ago. No one but the few mentioned above knew what pain we felt for her. (Only recently did we find out that many suspected but never hinted that they did).

BUT WE NEVER STOPPED LOVING HER.

We had many conversations amongst ourselves and with her as to what we did wrong as parents. Was it not keeping her in ballet classes and instead letting her become a soccer goalie? Maybe encouraging her interest in wearing her Dallas Cowboys football helmet when she was little? I tried to interest her in shopping and cooking and all the girlie stuff, but she was independent and enjoyed the things outdoors that the guys did. I was also a tomboy growing up, so I saw nothing wrong with that. Looking back, you doubt everything you did or did not do as a parent and evaluate the impact it may have had on her current situation. I asked myself, "What DID I do wrong? What would have made a difference?" I thought maybe I should not have put her in daycare the first three years of her life so I could have nurtured her more. Who knows what had impact or not? It was hard not to blame myself for things as they were now, but I learned eventually that assessing the source of blame was an exercise in futility and not effective for our current needs as a family.

We visited her as often as we could and always tried our best to keep the lines of communication open, and there was still a part of me that wanted to believe that all would be well again. I closed my eyes to the thought that she might not change and that she may not have a husband one day. All we could do was pray, love her, be there for her and encourage her the best we could.

Then one day Mike and I were returning from a trip to see her, and on the way home we talked at length about how or if we could help her. We prayed in silence and endured feelings of sadness as we traveled the 220 miles home. As we neared our home, God suddenly gave me a revelation of His reassurance that He heard us, and He was still in control. This revelation was in the form of another promise He had made many thousands of years ago to His people. I spotted a beautiful double rainbow hanging in the sky just a few blocks from our home. I have seen very few double rainbows in my entire life, so it was as if it were put there for me, just at the right moment, to reassure me of His love and faithfulness to me — a promise from Him that all would be well again one day. If not now, one day in the future she would return to His plan for her life. It gave me much hope and comfort.

We had to be patient and wait upon the Lord. Only God can change someone going through a struggle like this. All we could do was PRAY... and wait... and wait... and wait. But after much waiting and prayer, I CAN REJOICE NOW because HE DID answer our prayers!!! I thank Him and give Him the glory because today she is free, AND happily married to a wonderful man.

I could finally tell my sweet and devoted prayer warrior friend that her prayers had been answered just before she passed away.

I could finally talk to my own mom now. I no longer had to fear whether she "judged" my daughter for what I suspected she had already guessed to be different about her. I found out that she had known for years but didn't feel free to talk to me about it either. In fact, she emphasized how much she loved her no matter what. Oh, how we could have helped each other if we had felt the freedom to talk about this together. It's amazing how when your loved one who has been struggling with a secret sin finally feels the freedom to become open and honest about it, the openness becomes a catalyst to free all *their* loved ones who have also been protecting their secret. We create our own little prisons that keep us from getting the help we all need to deal with the issues at hand by keeping our secrets, even if those secrets are well intentioned to protect the ones we love. Instead, the secrecy just shuts down the lines of communication and resources for help. We live a life of deception as we try to maintain an appearance that all is well and we make excuses for their behaviors that appear out of the norm.

The "music" didn't come back to stay for long, but she did return for a year of healing and family restoration. We spent time together that had been robbed by our separation. When we were all strong again as a family, she moved back to her home in Austin. This time we parted company as a renewed family. The parting was the way it should have been many years ago. The music moved on down the highway to start fresh but a new song was in my heart as she left this time — a song of rejoicing and praise.

I am so proud of my daughter for enduring the battle and have always been proud of her, even as she struggled to be free. I rejoice with her in her victory and her desire to help others overcome this struggle. I know her heart has always been to serve and stand for God. I praise Him again for all He has brought her through! I pray He will give her strength to bring hope to others who want to fight for a life free from homosexuality or any kind of stronghold they may be facing.

May God grant the power of His truth and mercy and strength to anyone who wants to be free. Mothers, be strong for your daughters. Tell them and show them that you love them no matter what. Try to have that heart to heart talk sooner than later. Don't try to ignore it like I did or try to act like you are cool with that inappropriate relationship anymore than you would if it were a married man she was having an affair with. Pray to God for wisdom as a parent and for God to open the spiritual eyes of your loved one who is being deceived into embracing a lifestyle God never intended His creation to partake in. Claim the power in the Word of God when you feel weak and He will give you strength to overcome and endure. It is a slow process and much patience will be required.

Blessings on you as you travel this road to healing.

Dad's Story

Let me start with a disclaimer: The words I use to describe the "experience" of finding out my daughter was attracted to the same sex are anemic at best. Just as those who are suddenly blinded experience hypersensitivity in other senses such as hearing and smell, the realization that my "little girl" was in a very real spiritual struggle intensified everything in me. Words fall very short.

For at least a year, I had a foreboding feeling that our family was going to be challenged with a real crisis but I had no clue what to expect. There were families in our local church who were going through crises of cancer, death, divorce, and financial difficulties. We watched families going through very tough times and God was contrasting each of them with our family in my heart. We were not going through anything like this and God was making that point to me every Sunday as we prayed for them. There was a dread in me that God was letting me know to be ready. I believe God is more vocal in our lives than we give Him credit for.

I ignored and did not see the signals that my wife saw. She has always been intuitive but I did not want to hear the warnings and hints she was giving me. The reality of our crisis began for me the morning we confronted Christy while sitting on her bed.

My background is fairly standard. I'm an old guy, so as a child I was pretty naïve and unaware of homosexuality. Awareness came in the form of the other "education" one receives in school, and usually comes with all the opinions and prejudices of the "teachers." I was no exception.

I was not ready for this confirmation from my sweet daughter that she was attracted to other females. I had no idea what to say to her, what to do, or how to respond. At the point in our sobbing conversation on that bed, when she needed our comfort and re-assurance of our love, God's grace clearly cut through the pain, the confusion, the anger, the shame, and even my "education" to guide me to tell her that we were "simply going to love her through this." God's grace was sufficient for that moment for Sharon and I to communicate to Christy that our love for her remained intact and that while we did not know what the next minutes, hours, and days would bring, the spiritual bond of this family was not changed and we would engage together to see this through.

Life was suddenly not the same — never to be the same again. As soon as we finished praying with Christy and got off the bed, there was the reality of what to do. The option of returning to "normal" living was gone. As a man, a father, the spiritual head of the home, while feeling like the complete failure, I felt the immediate sense of urgency to get Christy help. We knew she remained at-risk by staying in the existing environment and that had to change.

At the same time, we knew we needed to do what was best for Christy, and recognizing that what she was going through spiritually and emotionally was far worse than anything we were going through. I was in shock! In an instant, my priorities and perspectives before our conversation were not my priorities and perspectives now. My core was shaken and I was experiencing a variety of extreme emotions by the minute that largely combined to condemn anything good in me. The questions were rolling through my heart and mind: How could I have so completely missed this? How had we raised this child so wrong that would lead her down this path? Why didn't she come to us sooner? Who can help her? What do we do now? Most of the answers were either never to come or would come much later.

Life was suddenly and clearly larger than me. It had exceeded my capacity and capability to "manage." I suddenly understood what it meant to pray unceasingly. My prayer had become the inarticulate "groaning" that is described in the Bible, and it was constantly rolling out of my heart seeking any relief from the pain.

Once again, God's grace was sufficient in the form of a Godly young couple who knew Christy, knew what she was experiencing, and offered to have her live with them in another city for a while. A good first step — thank you, Lord!

Christy left our home, the only home she had known, within a couple of days. It had not been the departure I had played out in my mind and expected before all this. It was not the blessing of watching my child go out on their own for the first time, fully prepared and equipped for life and the world. It was an unplanned, crisis-driven, desperate move to get our lovely daughter in a safe place, "God help us!" act. The father within me wanted to keep her home so we could help her and minister to her needs as a family, but we knew we could no longer be the only source of help for her. This was going to take God's intervention and we did not want to short circuit what seemed to be His moving in her life. My heart was broken.

Christy's revelations coupled with her sudden departure had the feel of our family being ripped apart in every way. We knew she was hurting and we were as well, including our son. There was an immediate need for us to understand what more we could do to support and help her, while helping each other, and understanding how we were going to explain her sudden departure from our home. For Christy, we began to search for Christian-oriented professional help but soon found out it was largely nonexistent. For us, because of the stigma associated with homosexuality, the need to protect our daughter and really not having anyone we felt comfortable sharing this with, we were effectively left to minister to each other.

The emotions and spiritual battles within in me were intense and constant. Hurt, fear, anger, sadness, disgust, shame, despair, and mostly condemnation were now all my constant "companions." Relief took the form of prayer and sleep. God had been merciful to us and His Holy Spirit now comforted me to help me get through each day — minute by minute. Sleep was not so merciful and life became a very poor distraction from the intense pain and guilt I was experiencing.

Foremost and constantly on my mind was the well being of my daughter. I knew she was hurting, lonely, and feeling like we had cast her aside. The sense of helplessness and (admittedly) hopelessness was overwhelming.

This would be the new normal for the first few years of this journey. We fell into a mode of calling and seeing Christy as often as we could (she moved several times) to reassure her of our love, encourage her, pray with her, and show our support. We tried to be good listeners while trying not to put her under any pressure from any expectations. Christy became a major barometer in my life. If she hurt, I hurt. If she was good, I was good. The prayers were constant that God would give her peace, clarity of mind, and would simply protect her. The pain of knowing that this spiritual battle was hers to wage internally alone was unbearable. It is not the nature of parents to "sit on the sidelines" when it comes to our kids, but in this case, the only thing our direct intervention would do is interfere with God's work and mess things up. Our best help for Christy was prayer, showing our love, and being there when she needed us.

To know Christy is to know that she is a very strong-willed and determined personality. She operates predominantly in a very rational environment and can give you the basis for any decision (large or small) that she makes in her life. She is non-conventional, focused, intelligent, loving, and very passionate about the Lord and making a difference in this world. I've always told myself, "If you want to debate her on any topic, make sure you come well armed."

It was her strengths coupled with her spiritual drive to know God and serve Him that I believe was the sustaining and driving force behind her transition to the lovely woman she is today. We have witnessed her years of intense personal and spiritual struggle, followed by periods of growth in strength and determination, followed most recently by seeing God work miracles in her life that included physical, spiritual, financial, and matrimonial. Dan is a Godly-walking miracle in our lives and we are so blessed to have him in our family. The more we get to know him, the greater the miracle becomes.

Over time, God has answered my prayers for Christy and He has mercifully ministered to me. He has taught me that He is at His strongest when I am at my weakest. I have witnessed hopeless deliver hope and accomplishment of the humanly impossible. I have experienced a depth of His mercy and grace that sufficiently met our immediate needs, and He delivered them at just the right time. Above all else, I have experienced a love that is forgiving, comforting, and transformational. He has taught me that we are all at risk in this world with its afflictions and that it is not for me to explain or defend. The only thing that has real power is His love and I am to not only love my daughter through her spiritual crises but also my wife, my son, and my neighbor. He has also taught me that there is no "opt out" clause in this life. He commanded us to love our neighbor unconditionally without condemnation or judgment. He didn't ask us.

To Parents of Young Children

Sharon and I soul-searched for years to understand where we may have gone wrong in raising Christy. We never came up with a legitimate cause and time has taught me that life's answers are not that simple. I believe anyone, young or old, is subject to any of life's myriad offering of afflictions. What God has revealed to us is that there was one very important thing we did right. We raised Christy in an environment that taught her who God is, about His love for her, and that Jesus covered all of us from our sin with His death on the cross. Beyond that, we were essentially spectators, encouragers, and prayer warriors for her during the last several years. It was God who touched Christy's heart early in life and gave her the passion to pursue Him in all things. It is that God-given passion that sustained and redeemed her through these years. Sharon and I give all glory to God for Christy, for her love and pursuit of Christ's will in her life, and her determination to fight.

Parents, equip your children in their early years for the crises that will enter their lives. I have always heard this, but the reality is that the worst-case conditions that accompany a crisis of faith or identity usually include your inability to exercise any control or even be heard by your child. Say what God places on your heart to tell your children early and often — while you are not in a critical situation and when your words will be received as instruction rather than perceived as confrontation. Plant these messages on their heart while they are young. Then, as they do go through traumatic turning points, you can ask God to raise these messages in their hearts. In this way, you are not only equipping your child, but you are "arming" yourself with an ability to speak to your child's heart through your prayers.

To Families of Loved Ones Involved in Homosexuality

I pray God's peace on your life. The reality of your situation may be like ours — that life will never be the same and that your precious child's circumstances may require years of loving endurance from everyone. This is a battle that requires you to be ready every day and will take you beyond human limits — if you wage it by yourself. I want to encourage you to set your mind to conquer the marathon, not win the sprint. I also want to reassure you that God's love and grace is so very capable to sustain you through it all. What you see as impossible is so easily possible with God. The life that will never be the same can be a life that is restored and rich with the fellowship with your loved one.

Lastly, you may struggle with reconciling your beliefs with the reality of your loved one's choices.

Recognize that reconciliation does not have to preclude the love you have for them. You do not have to compromise your beliefs, but you don't have to stop loving your child either. It is possible to do both.

Acknowledgments

The real accomplishment of this book is that stories like mine are possible. Without the regeneration of life in Christ, my story wouldn't exist. But after any birth, there is growing to do, and they say it takes a village to raise a child. Please, meet my village. Below are some of the major people who made my journey possible, (mostly) in chronological order.

Mom and Dad, thank you. Thank you for loving me, for being supportive as I've told my story, and for unashamedly stepping up to the mic with eager delight to add gravitas to my voice and credibility to the truth. You have been beautiful and courageous hearts, not only then, but now, as you open the window to share your insight. I am forever grateful.

Jon and Andrea, thank you for always loving me, and for giving me permission to share our family's story. Jon, you are the sweetest brother, full of maturity and strength. Your words of affirmation along the journey have carried me at times when you never could have known how much I needed to hear them. I love you and I am so proud of who you are.

Chantelle Macune, thank you for your prayer all of my life and for sowing into me and all of the girls in our Sunday School class. You engaged me in real conversations when I was just a kid, and helped instill in me a love for God's word that has held me all this time. It's such an honor to call you friend.

Angie and Bobby Cox, thank you for listening and opening your home to me. Angie, you were the first ears to hear my cry, and I could not be more grateful for your gracious responses and genuine belief in me in those early days. Bobby, thank you for giving me the opportunity to lead Bible studies in our youth group and live out some of my calling even when I was so young. You gave me a taste of what made this fight worth it, and I was forever ruined in the best of ways.

Betty McGinty, thank you for reaching out to me and teaching me about the Holy Spirit. Thank you for all the late night phone calls and the patient re-listening to all of my anguish and heartbreak when it was so fresh, and I was so young and afraid and alone in Dallas. Most importantly, thank you for teaching me about covenant, and friendship, and about "putting one foot in front of the other" even when I didn't feel like it. You made my darkest days bright.

Gail Long, thank you for seeing something worth holding onto in me, even when many could not. You picked me up when I needed it most, and I am forever grateful. I moved on in my pursuit of freedom because the long talks, longer emails, and rich discussion over prophetic revelation gave me a greater mystery to chase, a higher cause to fight for. And to all the Freedom's Fire team, thank you for loving me and walking with me this far.

Bob and Leslie Long, and Karen Serna, thank you for standing in faith for my healing when I first moved to Austin. I will never forget the nights of prayer and soaking (Kevin Prosch!) and ministry that made Austin feel like home, and for that you will always have my honor. Bob, you believed in me and instilled a passion for the kingdom of God that will stay with me forever, and I'm grateful to call you friend.

Allison Gephardt, thank you for being a true friend. Our conversations and your humorous honesty have helped me frame my words with holy boldness. You keep it real, and it gives me strength to speak.

Hope Taylor, thank you for convincing gentlemen still exist. I needed to know that when I was still afraid of men. Also, your constant diplomacy, tact, and honor in dealing with all people has set the bar for how I wish to interact with culture. Your love for our nation has been an inspiration to me. We have work to do together, and like you say to all of us young people, I now say to you, "I won't do this without you."

Dana Sleger, thank you for your friendship and for your inspiration to me to always be a greater thinker and writer than I think I could be. You give me something to chase down by your mere existence. You share my love of C.S. Lewis, you know when it's time to party, and more importantly, you've been a real friend. Like you say, "you're a lifer." I'm so thankful for you. Oh yeah, and thanks for editing this book!

Darrell and Allison Vesterfelt, thank you for letting me be part of the *Prodigal Magazine* team, for believing in me, and for giving me a platform to amplify the message of hope God has burned into my bones. And all the *Prodigal Magazine* writers, thank you for helping me spread this message of hope and for your friendship. So many lives are going to be forever marked with heaven because of this group of incredibly talented writers. You guys are a precious gift and it's such an honor to be among you.

To my Writing Prayer Team — thank you for opening your inboxes up to me, and for praying and standing with me when I've been tired or had writer's block. I can forgo appearances and whine a little bit with you guys and you always reply with perfect encouragement. I'm excited about the victories we've already seen together and eager for what's to come.

They say to save the best for last...

Dan, my heart... thank you for letting me violate routines, stay up late, and sometimes be an earless wonder as I tune out the world and write. Your belief in my writing, your unashamed promotion of my testimony, and your unending emotional strength are all now necessary to my ability to pick up a pen. You're the stuff they used to make husbands out of in the good old days, and I'm glad you picked me to be your wife. I believe in you right back. We're just getting started, and I know you're going to take us to amazing places. Thank you for being so much like Jesus. You give me something to strive for with every word I speak. I love you forever.

About the Author

Christy McFerren is a writer, blogger and speaker on the topics of faith and culture. Her blog, *Living a Thoughtful Revolution* (http://christymcferren.com), is focused on exploring what it means to thoughtfully live out the answers Jesus gave us to the questions culture is asking. She is also a featured content writer for *Prodigal Magazine* (http://prodigalmagazine.com) where she writes stories at the intersection of Church and Culture.

In addition to writing and speaking, Christy and her husband Dan run a brand development firm called Thoughtful Revolution. They offer web design and development, brand identity, content authoring and marketing services with a special focus on writers and authors. You can find out more about their services at thoughtfulrevolution.com.

Christy and Dan live in Austin, TX.

Twitter: @christymcferren
Facebook: facebook.com/ChristyMcFerrenWriter
Email: christy@christymcferren.com

FirstStepsOut.com

FirstStepsOut.com was built as a place of refuge for parents and friends and family in search of better ways to support their loved ones who struggle with homosexuality. This is not a professional counseling group and no one is paid for the time they spend in conversation here. We're just a group of people helping people. We have a policy to protect the privacy of all group members and to never take any discussions outside the forum to protect the privacy and dignity of those we love. Please visit the website and refer people you know who need help. It is our vision that the Church will be a place of reformed perspective on how to handle homosexuality. We want to see the Church become a haven for those seeking healing, and the wounded healers who join in this dialogue will become the pioneers of a new era of engagement and response that brings both truth and hope.

Made in the USA
San Bernardino, CA
17 November 2012